SURVIVAL UNDER THE SUN

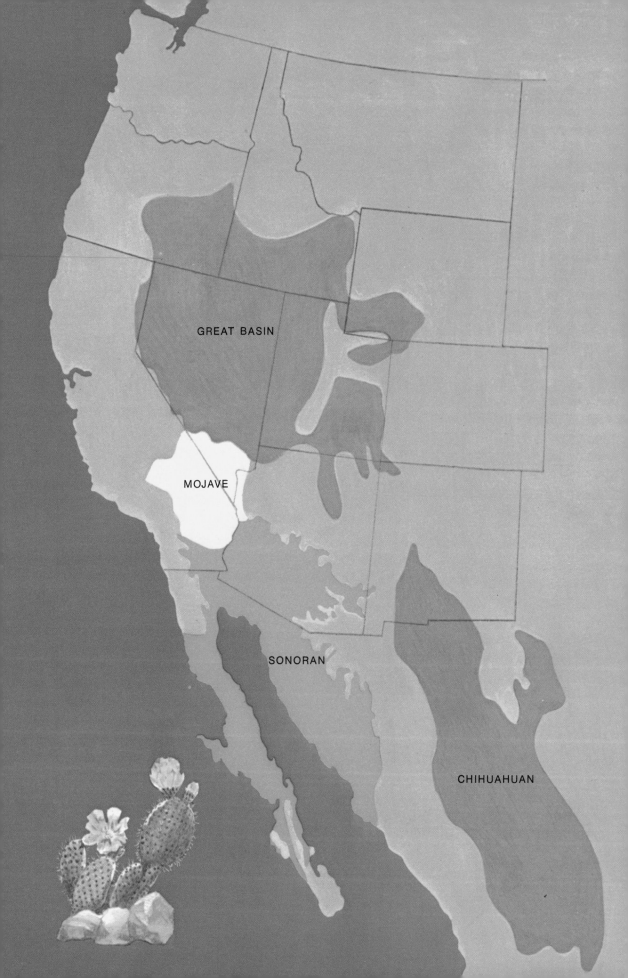

Marlin Perkins' Wild Kingdom

SURVIVAL UNDER THE SUN

LEWIS WAYNE WALKER

With an Introduction by Marlin Perkins

Illustrated by Jean Zallinger

Doubleday & Company, Inc., Garden City, New York

Acknowledgment

This book is based on an original story developed for an episode of the internationally known television series, *Wild Kingdom*, and I am deeply grateful for the research assistance and continued support graciously given me by the staff of Don Meier Productions, producers of this outstanding program.

Especially I want to thank Don Meier himself for his invaluable creative guidance and generous editing efforts in the expansion of the original story into this full-length book.

LEWIS WAYNE WALKER

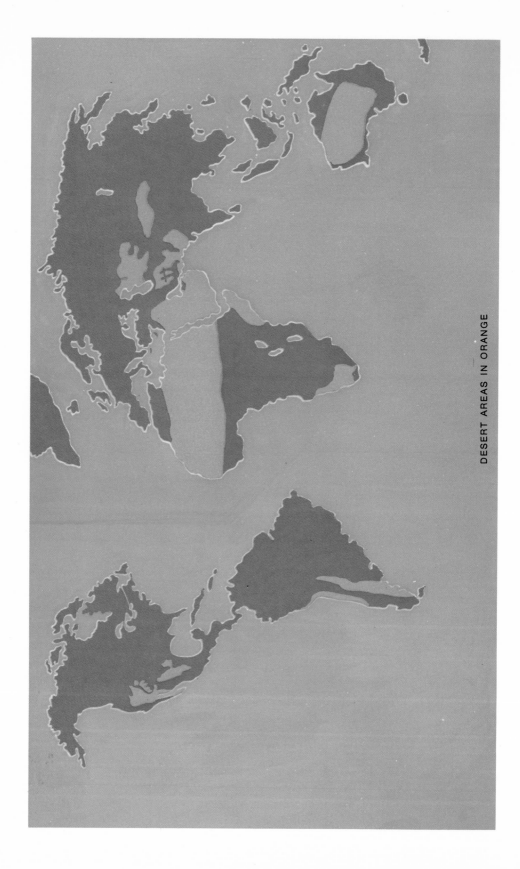

DESERT AREAS IN ORANGE

Introduction

If the human population of the world were evenly divided, one out of every seven persons would be living on a desert. Much of our time would be spent fighting extremes of temperature, the cold of night, and the desiccating heat of the day. Throughout most of each year, the quest for sufficient water would be an overwhelming problem; and then a month or two would come when the skies would open, wetting the parched land in a short reprieve from its customary harshness.

Fourteen per cent of the world's land area fits the requirements to put it into this arid desert category, and as a result it is only in comparatively recent years that the technology of modern man has made deserts tolerable for any but the hardiest members of the human race. A few of the gadgets that man has recently designed for both comfort and survival are really not new at all. Many are copies of natural adaptations that have had eons of use on the deserts of the world by the plants and wild life that call the deserts home.

This, then, is the story of one of the harshest, yet one of the most beautiful parts of the wild kingdom—the desert.

Marlin Perkins

Contents

SNOWY OWL

POLAR BEAR

MOOSE

ARCTIC HARE

ARCTIC FOX

WOLVERINE

BISON

BLACK BEAR

GRAY WOLF

BROWN
JACK RABBIT

MOUNTAIN
PLOVER

BROWN COYOTE

PACIFIC OCEAN

KIT FOX

KANGAROO
RAT

ATLANTIC OCE

Chapter 1

This Desert Land

On the mountains and in the valleys of the temperate regions of our American West, tremendous trees flaunt large leaves which cast shadows over dark trunks and onto the dark earth below. If rocks exist they are hidden beneath a thick layer of mulch, the accumulation of decaying plant life laid down through countless centuries. The animals that walk these tree-lined corridors are as black as the shadows they pass through. Those that are eaten by others are dark, the better to escape their enemies; while those that do the eating are also dark, the better to enable them to approach their prey.

That, in essence, is survival in its most rudimentary form. Variations of it can be found on all the different topographies of the world. White bears, white foxes, white owls, and white rabbits inhabit the snow and ice fields of the North. A little farther south, where temperatures permit brush and stunted trees to grow for a few short months of the year, there are ptarmigan, weasels, and rabbits that have changeable coats— white in winter, brown in summer.

From the dark forests of the Canadian border country emerge the grassy plains, almost shadowless because of the dearth of trees, but covered with a carpet of sun-baked grasses. Here the light brown prairie dogs blend with the soil and vegetation so that only their movements give a clue to their location. There are jack rabbits, long-legged, fleet-of-foot creatures that in this flat land of few hiding places have developed speed as well as color to escape their many enemies.

Yet in the Southwest, a land of extremes where virtually everything is different, practically all life is modified or adapted to such an extent that some of the creatures and plants have lost almost all similarity to their cousins living in other environments. Even if we travel on other continents we find similar patterns of color. It is as though the world were ringed with latitudinal bands creating a similarity of plants and animals best fitting the regions in which they live.

At one time this matching of life to the terrain on which it lived was considered spontaneous creation. This was believed for centuries until an Austrian monk named Gregor Johann Mendel let his curiosity get the better of existing dogma. By breeding slightly different varieties of plants together, he found that there were some characteristics that could be lost and others that could be retained and strengthened. He proved that most minor variations which occasionally crop up in all living things could be inherited by their offspring.

If the variation was detrimental to survival, the animal's death would prevent the trait from being passed to future generations. But if it were advantageous, this trait would in time become the rule rather than the exception. Later, Darwin called it the "survival of the fittest." However, "fittest" can have several interpretations. In the wild kingdom, where every organism strives to stay alive, it means the ability to escape enemies, to get food, to catch its prey. It is survival by any means that permits the propagation of the species.

What is best for survival on a certain type of terrain in one part of the world seems to be best on similar terrain in another part of the world. With this in mind scientists have used the term "parallel evolution" to explain the phenomena of widely separated and non-related plants and animals that have similar characteristics. And as all life strives to exist, parallel paths on widely separated deserts have often reached the same goal, creating look-alikes in both plants and animals, even though a common ancestry never existed.

Look-alikes exist in deserts too, even though their birth and their continued existence could be due to any number of different circumstances. California's Mojave Desert, for instance, is of the rain-shadow type for it is hidden from the prevailing westerly winds by high coastal mountains. These ranges are an effective blockade to the moisture picked up over the Pacific. Clouds, upon encountering the western slopes, have a tendency to discharge water, and by the time they pass over the crests are no longer humid—having left their loads on the pines, oaks, and other growths that need the abundant rain to survive. As a result the eastern sides of the mountains are comparatively barren, with cacti and other drought-resistant plants occupying the same altitudes that have the pines and oaks on the ocean side.

Where this mountain rain shadow occurs on some of the deserts of the Northern Hemisphere, observers in high airplanes can see a sharp line of demarcation. It is almost as though a surveyor had drawn the line and botanists had come in, planting dark green plants on the western slopes, light tan on the eastern. In the Southern Hemisphere, however, the prevailing winds travel from east to west, and there, the few deserts of rain-shadow origin give proof to the shadow theory by being on the west side of the mountains instead of the east.

Another cause of deserts is the vertical movement of moisture-bearing clouds. If the movement is upward, condensation and subsequent rain results, but if downward, there is a drying effect and precipitation is withheld from the ground. There are a few deserts uncontrolled by any of these factors, so that in some areas moisture-laden air tends to lose its load of water if forced

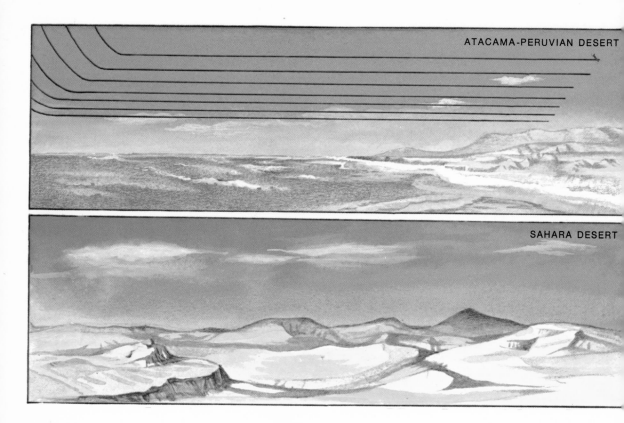

SAHARA DESERT

over long distances. The interior areas of Australia and of Africa's Sahara are of this type.

The Sahara, largest of all deserts, covers three million square miles of land (an area almost as large as the entire United States) and stretches completely across North Africa. The second largest is the Australian Desert, which occupies over 40 per cent of that country. Although its most arid regions are located in the central and western portions, in reality there is only a comparatively narrow belt of coast line that does not adhere to the scientific classification of what constitutes a desert.

At one time a desert was classified as any area that received less than ten inches of rainfall per year. This hard and dry rule included in the category bits of the snow-covered arctic which are obviously not deserts in any sense of the word in its present usage. As it stands now, there are restrictions that limit deserts in other ways and tend to place them between the latitudes of

14

TAKLA-MAKAN DESERT

MOJAVE DESERT

fifteen and forty degrees north of the equator, and fifteen and forty degrees south of the equator.

Strangely, the actual equatorial belt lying between fifteen degrees north and fifteen degrees south has only a few desert areas. They are minor protuberances from existing deserts extending across its borders. This dearth of desert land on the equator may seem incongruous. By location it would seem that its encircling belt should be as hot as any area, but converging air currents from north and south create vertical winds which promote a great deal of rain. It is the meeting of these forces that gives birth to tropical storms such as hurricanes, typhoons, and chubascos, so although some conditions are right for deserts, the ten-inch limit on rainfall is exceeded, making desert land a rarity.

Wladimir Köppen of the University of Graz in Austria originated a mathematical system of temperature and precipitation figures to determine what is desert and what is not. By utilizing his formula (and this takes a mathematical genius) where readings of wind currents—or the lack of them—are compared with readings of rainfall, runoff, ground absorption, and mountain ranges, conditions in widely separated parts of the world have their similarities explained.

Although most deserts are the result of readily explained natural causes that have existed for ages, there are some that owe at least a little of their aridity to the work of man, both ancient and modern. Excavations on some parts of the Sahara have revealed a tremendous series of irrigation canals as well as buried towns, proving that these areas once had a human population much greater than the land could possibly support at present.

In ancient days there was a ground cover made up of plants which rejuvenated the soil, holding it in place and preventing a runoff of loam. But this ground cover might have had a bearing on climate also, for after the plants were cleared off by the ancients, sunshine struck the surface of the earth creating an area where the sun's rays would be released as heat into the ground. This absorption and release which occurred in the past created updrafts, and these updrafts carried moisture with them. As the lift of moisture-laden air caused condensation and rainfall, some of the deserts of today were verdant areas in the past. Then man cleared the plants away. Without the dark cover, the sun's rays would be reflected away with almost no change in temperature—as happens in those same areas today.

In the last half century, a man-made desert was well on the way to being formed in the United States and the mistakes which started the land in its regression were similar to those which created part of the Sahara. This was the dust bowl of the West Central United States which, after supplying wheat to the entire world throughout two world wars, began to show the effect of overwork. The constant cultivation gave the land no chance to rest, and eliminated any possibility for roots to bind together. When winds blew, dust—the nutrient of the soil, was carried away in clouds. Only the heavier sand and gravel were left in place. This erosion not only made the sandy areas unproductive but also ruined regions on the lee side by starting dunes of dust that smothered everything in their paths.

Many years of scientific doctoring by soil specialists and millions of dollars were expended before this overworked land was again made productive. If immediate action had not been taken, that 14 per cent figure for the deserts of the world would now be slightly larger and the world's ability to feed a ballooning population slightly smaller.

Although a few million years seem like a long time to human beings who crowd so much into less than a century, it is infinitesimal in the world's geological history. So, by that standard, our present-day deserts are comparatively new in the world, having been started from one to five million years ago. Prior to those days many areas that are now dry were probably verdant with tremendous forests and streams. Petrified trees, oil deposits, and underground coal point to a climate that no longer exists.

Just what it was that caused these changes is not definitely known, but of the theories advanced, those of volcanic action or shrinkage of the earth's crust seem most logical. Either one, or a combination of both, could create mountain ranges and deep depressions not only on dry land but also beneath the surface of the ocean. Shrinkage of the earth's crust could force warm or cold water currents on predictable paths and thus cause atmospheric updrafts or downdrafts along coast lines. The above-water mountain ranges would do the same with wind currents, making them dump their moisture on certain areas and withhold it from others.

Whether these changes were cataclysmic or long-drawn-out is also unknown, but it is certain that life in the regions that became arid had their ecology so disrupted that little if any life survived. Plants that once lived in the areas of bountiful rainfall could not adapt, so they died. Animals living in an almost marshy terrain not only found their adaptations useless in this new climate, but with vegetation gone they succumbed to starvation. In a general way each "new" desert started through trial and error to develop a new interrelated community. As far as life was concerned, the desert had become a vacuum, and new plants and animals began to fill this vacuum.

For the sake of continuity, pretend that these deserts were sterile—nothing but rocks and sand with all nutrients eliminated by the forces which changed them from what they were. And then guess how the vacuum would have been filled in a similar area of the present day. With no decaying of disintegrated plant life in the soil, most of the plants, as we know them now, would not get a foothold without a long conditioning period as a starter. In this conditioning, primitive plants called lichens would probably be the first to move in. Some lichens are so tiny that to an unaided eye they seem more like stains than living organisms. Naturally the gonidia by which they propagate are smaller still and practically weightless. Tests have shown that they are in the atmosphere all over the world and were, for example, the first bit of plant life to gain a foothold on the volcanic island of Krakatoa after it exploded so violently in 1883.

Chapter 2

Some Plants of the Desert

The relentless, ever-present sun beat down upon the arid ground of the desert. Yet rains occasionally fell, perhaps once a year, perhaps only once every several years. But with the rain the desert had a reprieve. Every time there was a dampening of any type, some of the lichen spores were grounded and commenced to grow, pulling chemicals from the rocks and transforming energy from the sun. Even though these first plants were so thin they could not be seen by the naked eye, they—in time—formed an absorbent surface permitting the rocks to retain a little more moisture than they had had before. So, through the centuries, layer after layer was added after each rain. With each bit of growth, minerals were drawn from the rock and deposited as a shiny coating which, on the deserts of the world, is now called "desert varnish."

By examining some of the old man-made structures in the world, one can see how long the building of this varnish coating took. The pyramids of Egypt, for instance, show it but faintly, and in our own Southwest some of the rock drawings (petro-

PICTOGRAPH INTERPRETED AS A MAN ATTACKED BY AN ELEPHANT
(HAVASUPAI CANYON)

glyphs) made by long-gone Indians were achieved by scratching the varnish and exposing the true color of the rocks beneath. Only a few of these scratches, even those made over a thousand years ago, show any noticeable build-up of varnish despite their age.

One of the strangest uses of desert varnish is to be found along the shores of the Colorado, where this mighty river carves its way through the Mojave. There, on plateaus a hundred feet above the high-water mark, the outlines of tremendous reclining human figures have been left by an ancient Indian race.

The system used by these primitive peoples for leaving traces of their occupancy, although simple, would have been impossible if centuries of lichens had not set the stage. By the lichens' action of blackening the sides and tops of the rocks and leaving the undersides untouched, each stone was two-toned. All the Indians had to do was invert the stones to mark, for centuries

20

to come, the figurine outlines they wished to show. But even so, their task was an ambitious one, for some of the figures exceed one hundred feet in length. Just why they were made is unknown. Perhaps they had a now-forgotten religious significance or perhaps it was just an aborigine's way of saying "I was here."

As these hardy lichens set the stage for the petroglyphs, they also were the beginning of other desert growths. The lichens enriched the soil by pulling necessary chemicals from the rocks and making it a receptive growing place for other plants to get a foothold. Probably thousands of plant species moved in but only a few hardy ones survived. Most of those that did have descendants so adapted to the environment that they no longer resemble their original pioneering forebears. In a general way, their adaptations to make life possible in these arid environments have placed them in one of two categories, drought resisters or drought evaders. In the latter class are most of the flowering annuals that bloom for a month or so, scatter their seeds, and barely leave a trace of their occupancy throughout the rest of the year.

That old unanswerable question—which came first, the chicken or the egg—could well be changed to which came first, the plant or the seed. As the seeds of many desert annuals have a much longer life than the parent plants, their many adaptations

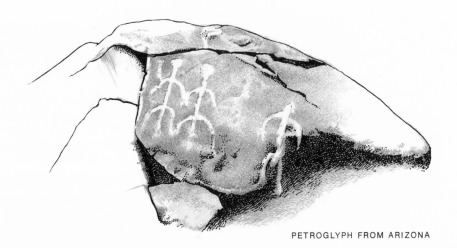

PETROGLYPH FROM ARIZONA

to ensure species survival are really more interesting than the blooms that live for a moment, then wither and die. At this point we shall investigate the dispersal of the seeds, and their means of being scattered over a desert. Some seeds have evolved systems whereby there is a better-than-even chance of landing in a favorable area. We shall find that desert animals play a most important role in the moving of seeds from place to place.

One of the strangest seed pods to be found on the desert is the devil's claw—a brownish branchlike structure roughly bent into the shape of an open-ended heart. At the lower pointed end there is a thickened fiber which is used by the plant as a seed container. At the upper open end, separated by an inch or so of space, there are two needle-sharp claws pointing toward the center of the so-called heart. The entire contraption has a spring steel resiliency which works like a trap keeping it in a set position.

22

Growing as it does in dry stream beds where the moisture content of the soil is slightly higher than on the flat areas nearby, the devil's claw naturally grows on active game trails. Any deer or other hoofed animal is liable to scuffle a hoof into the open end of the claw and have the two sharp points imbed themselves in the hock. As the animal moves, it scatters seeds until wear and tear finally breaks the pod apart. By this system, seed dispersal is not only widespread but tends to occur where the chances of moisture are better than normal, for most hoofed animals seek water holes at least once a day.

Several desert annuals disperse their seeds by using a gluelike substance on sticky stems. The spiderling, a crawling threadlike plant, breaks at the slightest touch and, by means of a mucilage with which it is liberally coated, sticks to anything that touches it. If it is a deer, fox, coyote, or any other large animal that caused the pieces to break and cling to the animal, some seeds ride for miles before drying winds ruin the adhesive and let the hitchhiking seeds drop to the ground where they grow into plants.

Desert mistletoe, although not an annual, uses the same system to obtain a foothold in the crotch of a branch where it then grows and parasitizes a tree. The mistletoe, however, actually "pays for its ride" by producing edible berries which are the sought-after food of numerous birds. In this way, it serves a double purpose. The berries, which stick to the beak or throat feathers are rubbed off on a branch during the birds' normal periods of preening. Even those that are swallowed retain the capability of germination despite the fact that digestive juices have removed the tasty outer coating.

Some botanists feel that this ability to resist digestive juices, combined with the germination of non-swallowed seeds, has a definite bearing on the mistletoe's survival. It is supposed that those seeds retaining the sticky coating have a longer germination period than those with the coating gone and in actual contact with the branch. If humidity conditions are right when the seeds are dropped, the uncoated seeds may take hold and grow, but if the correct weather conditions are delayed, then those with the outer coating may be the ones to survive.

Anyone who has walked through desert valleys during the short period when summer rains have brought about a growth of desert grasses, has had his ankles pestered by the fruits of the three-awn grass. If the fruits were placed under a microscope, the enlargement would show a thin shaft tipped on one end with a tiny cone-shaped coil spring, sharply pointed like a carpenter's miniature auger. At the other end three small wings protrude outward at an angle set to catch the slightest breeze.

When the tiny seed pod is dropped by the wind onto the ground, it lands with its auger end in the porous sand. As the breeze blows across the desert, the tiny point will have found an opening and the shaft will rise to a vertical position. With each gust of air it will thread itself downward as though attempting to bury itself.

Experimentally the system can be made to work rapidly, but on the variable floor of the deserts many days would be utilized to accomplish the same result. Countless seeds would fail entirely blocked in the downward motion by impervious pebbles, or by becoming wedged sideways in such a way that no matter how many turns were made, a receptive foothold in the ground could not be attained. This system is part of the wonders of nature. It was developed through trial and error and not through any thought process. The few best suited to succeed pass on their suitabilities while millions of others never get the chance to pass on their faults.

The desert has another plant which, although unrelated to the three-awn grass, uses the same system to ensure the best germination, but its action is a little more positive. This is the filleree that places its branches flat on the ground, forming a circle of pancake size. Its seed pods are similar to those of the

three-awn grass, but by putting it under a magnifying glass, it will be seen that a series of tiny hairs have been added to the spiraling auger. The hairs point in one direction, positioned in such a way that once penetration into the sand is started, the seed cannot work itself loose.

The natural ability of living things to increase the possibility of survival will never cease to be a wonder to naturalists. No doubt the invention of the threaded screw was done on a drawing board in a relatively short time. Nature achieved the same goal but its progression took considerably longer. Someone dreamed up the lock nut, but it was not original, for the filleree with its tiny hairs had actually earned the patent centuries ago.

An interesting example of how man's inventions have followed nature is the invention, at the beginning of this century, by a manufacturer of farm machinery revolutionizing the planting of seed grain. The innovation was a tremendous grain-filled

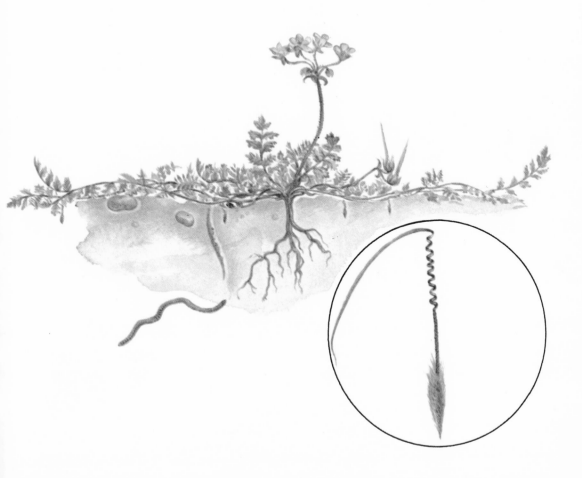

drum, drawn across a plowed field by a team of horses. With
each rolling revolution, rows of holes would come in contact
with the ground and a grain or so of wheat, barley, or oats
would drop to a spot where it would later grow.

If plants could hire attorneys the patent issued would have
been termed an infringement, because at least two desert plants,
one a native of this country and one introduced from Russia,
have been using this system from time immemorial. One of
these, the Russian plant, is known as the tumbleweed, a name
which pretty well describes its method of seed dispersal. Winter
or spring rains cause a rapid germination of tumbleweed seeds
and before many weeks have passed the resultant bushes take
on their characteristic ball-shaped form. All through the summer

months they continue to grow, often attaining a height and width of six or more feet. With the chilling winds of fall, however, the dark green foliage fades to dirty brown. When the prickly seed pods are ripe for sowing, the entire plant disconnects from the root at ground level. Then commences a rolling, bouncing journey that may go on for miles. Each wind-induced bounce plants a future generation in a sowing system that is not stopped until an immovable barricade impedes the progress.

So far our attention has been mainly centered on the drought evaders, those plants that do not show their stems aboveground in a daring attempt to challenge months of arid heat. Throughout most of the year they are virtually non-existent, with survival dependent on tiny seeds that patiently wait until the correct conditions for growing are co-ordinated. Then they grow rapidly, burst into bloom, scatter their offspring, and disappear once again. That old facetious admonition that says that a person should work eight hours, sleep eight hours, and play eight hours —but not the same eight hours, cannot be applied to these plants that survive by evading drought. Many, waiting for conditions to be just right, spend years underground, appear for a few weeks, and then wither and die.

Some desert plants, instead of remaining as seeds during periods of dryness, actually resist the desert sun and stay aboveground year after year. Those in this resister category are not only hardy in appearance but many have evolved almost unbelievable specialties to permit survival. And their specialties are not confined to seed dispersal but are spread over the entire plant all the way from underground root systems to impervious coatings on their outermost leaves. Living and thriving in areas where the ten or less inches of annual rainfall would make most growth dry up and blow away, these specialists have evolved a

variety of ways not only to conserve moisture but also to make the best use of what little is available.

Botanical authorities have estimated that an acre of corn takes from the soil and then releases into the air approximately three hundred thousand gallons of water in a short growing season. This is called transpiration and is as necessary to growing plants as the circulatory system in our bodies. However, some plants can afford to be wasteful if they live in areas where rainfall is abundant. As most of this transpired water exudes through the foliage, the wasteful ones are usually adorned with such large and beautiful leaves that the main trunk and its branches are almost hidden from sight. On the almost waterless western deserts, however, the luxury of leaves—as most people know them—was lost ages ago when trees first invaded the arid land. So instead of seeing trees on a desert densely clothed in foliage, most of them are stark bare with trunks and branches cutting sharp silhouettes against the sky line.

On some deserts even these trunks and branches are radi-

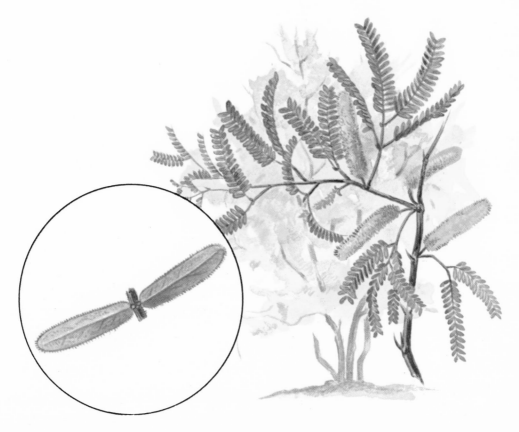

Desert plants with small leaves can circumvent moisture losses to survive.

cally different from those found in wetter climates. The customary gnarled brown or black bark is smooth and green. Many of the boughs are armored with spines and sharp hooks all the way to their tips, which makes even accidental contact extremely painful. Here we have a whole series of adaptations, each one a most necessary complement to another. If we go way back in history and theorize, perhaps we can make a fairly accurate guess on how these drastic changes gradually evolved.

There are two possibilities. One presumes that our present deserts were once much wetter than they are today, and the coal and oil now present beneath some of them, along with petrified trees, makes this presumption most logical. If the change from wet to dry was a gradual change that occupied ages of time, the growth from previous centuries had time to adjust. In this adaptive period some of the trees grew with slightly smaller leaves than others from the same crop of seeds, and in this drying climate they became the hardy ones and those previously normal became the misfits.

To understand this reasoning there are several basic facts about all life that must be known. The first of these is that nature is never stingy in the production of possible progeny, always producing many more than can possibly live. As examples, think of the salmon that lay thousands of eggs, the quail that have been known to lay over eighty eggs in a single season, the ear of corn where each kernel is a possible plant which could produce many ears.

The second rule is that no two living organisms are similar in every way. They might seem so to us—as alike as peas in a pod—but the differences are there. Some may be so infinitesimal that they could not be detected without several generations of selective breeding. Others might be as glaring as the albinos that occur once in every twenty or thirty thousand human births. Combined with these first two rules, the abundance of offspring which creates a surplus and the inherent differences in every living thing, there is a third which still works in wilderness areas on plants and the lower forms of animals.

This third rule concerns the elimination of the surplus which not only tends to keep the population of the world in balance but also leaves only the fittest stock as breeders to carry on and improve their race. In comparatively recent years the giant strides in medicine and technology have thwarted these natural laws as far as human beings are concerned, whether wisely or not only the future can tell.

The trees which were found in the desert grew slightly smaller leaves than others from the same crop of seeds. With less surface area there was a corresponding decrease in the transpiration of moisture and in periods of extreme drought they were able to survive while their larger leafed relatives could not. Here was selective breeding brought about by weather and not by predation, as is usually the case with animals.

However, this loss in the size of leaves created problems, for with the lessening of green chlorophyl exposed to the sun, photosynthesis was retarded. Without it, plants would die, for through its action the water from the ground, the gases from the atmosphere, and the energy from the sun separate the plant's liquid into hydrogen and oxygen. Some of the oxygen gas passes out of the plant through the same pores in the leaves that lets carbon dioxide from the atmosphere come in. When this dioxide is combined with hydrogen, sugar is formed which supplies the basic energy for life.

In this chemical process green chlorophyl is an absolute necessity. With the shrinkage of the leaves, the chlorophyl had to be replaced on some other part of the plant and somewhere in the eons of evolutionary development it shifted to the outside layer. So now on the western deserts we have a tree known by the Mexican name of *palo verde* which when translated means "green stick." Its leaves are tiny, so small in fact that when viewed from a short distance the main trunk and branches are seemingly leafless. And yet, the plant is as green as an eastern lawn.

All during the evolutionary period when the palo verde was

developing specialties for desert living, other plant species—by trial and error—were approaching the same end. Some began to shed their leaves completely and withdraw into a suspended state of dormancy during periods of extreme dryness. Others developed a shiny coating of a waxlike substance on their leaves. A few developed fuzzy hairs to protect the "stomata," the little openings on the underside of the leaf, through which transpiration takes place. These hairs tended to insulate the leaves from hot breezes which would increase evaporation. The wax coating achieved the same results but in a different way, for its purpose was to reflect the sun's rays before heat could be developed.

A few of the plants, on losing their gnarled protective bark, became susceptible as food for animals. But some of them developed distasteful sap which discouraged their attackers. Others achieved immunity by developing sharp spines, not as vicious as those found on cacti, but mean enough to make other foods a little more palatable.

But ingenius as these specialties are, there are others even more unbelievable. The greasewood or creosote bush, for instance, has seemingly developed a system whereby it cannot be crowded out by others of its own kind. For many years, desert travelers have remarked about its growth, a growth so evenly spaced that a valley of the bushes gives the impression of being planted with human aid. Recent research, however, discloses that the root tips of each individual plant permeate the nearby soil with an inhibitor which discourages the germination of the plant's own seeds.

There is some evidence that rainfall in excess of ten inches makes these bushes grow closer together, and in areas of less rainfall they are spaced farther apart. In a very general way this causes the limiting of offspring to a number that can happily survive in a special environment. The variable spacing of the plants, which is controlled by rainfall, is proof of the importance of water. If rainfall is heavy, the inhibitors are diluted and leached away; if rainfall is light, they remain in the soil and

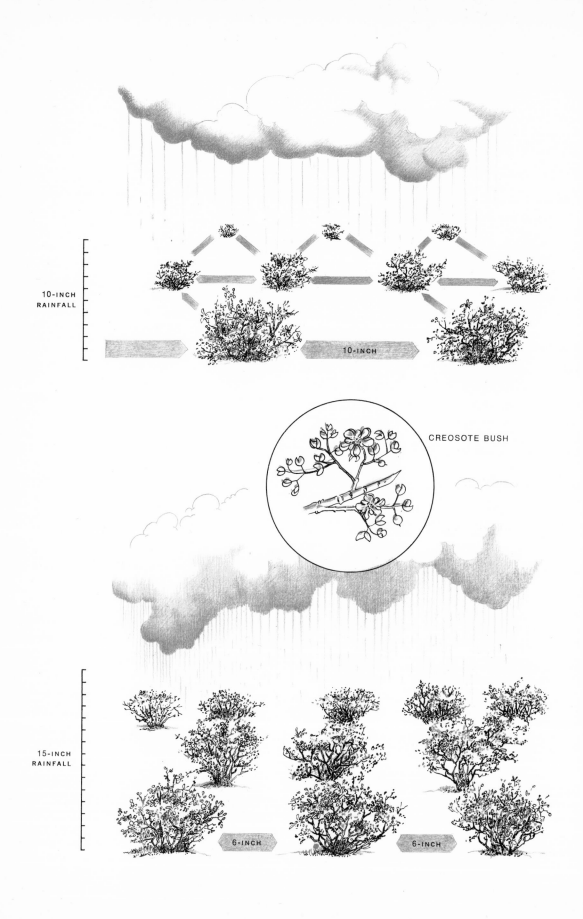

10-INCH
RAINFALL

10-INCH

CREOSOTE BUSH

15-INCH
RAINFALL

6-INCH

6-INCH

give a greater runoff surface upon which the parent plant can survive.

The germination of the seeds of the smoke tree was an enigma to botanists for many years. Even though these scientists took the sands from the desert washes where the wild plants flourished, and maintained a typical desert temperature and a controlled water supply in a greenhouse, smoke tree seedlings would not start. The secret was learned by accident when seeds that had bounced around in a car for weeks were planted and bushes resulted. The nurserymen learned they must file through the shell of the seeds before planting them.

In most areas of the world, seeds that need an abrasive action to commence their growth would never germinate. Where smoke trees grow, however, there are areas by-passed by all rainfall for months and sometimes years at a time. And when it does come down it is usually in the form of a torrential downpour. Dry washes fill to their brims and before the rushing waters settle into the parched sands, they sometimes travel twenty or thirty miles from where the rains fell. Smoke tree seeds picked up on the way are bounced from rock to rock, scraped over sand, and finally—scratched and scarred—rest in a depression where moisture conditions are right for growing. The seed's covering is its timer, set to release life only when moisture conditions are right from soaking rains that rarely occur.

With the water-caused abrasion and an assured dampness that extends downward many feet, a tiny rootlet bursts from the seed and grows. In the beginning months the new plant grows into the ground so that, on the surface, there is little evidence of the plant. It is almost as though the new taproot follows the rapidly receding waters that are necessary for life. After threading its way between boulders for a distance of several yards, the tiny branches, which appear aboveground, start to expand. But their growth is minimal—only a tiny fraction compared to what is happening underground. After about four years, the water-beaten seed will have transformed into a bush eight to ten inches across and a little over a foot in height.

This ratio of taproot to surface growth in smoke trees is hard to prove as they grow in the shifting sands of stream beds and excavations are difficult. However, the mesquite, which reaches a top size of about fifteen feet, often grows in mineralized areas. Its roots have been encountered in mine tunnels at a depth of over one hundred twenty-five feet—still going downward. Some of these lengthy taproots actually reach a water source deep underground since even in the driest of years occasional trees remain a little greener than their neighbors.

But, as not all plants are able to seek water at subterranean levels, there are some that absorb it when it is available and store it for months and sometimes years. One of the strangest of these is the so-called "century plant," a large plant that does not seem to have a set blooming season. Its gray-green leaves growing to a length of five feet or more are about an inch thick and about ten inches wide. They radiate from the heart (or center) of the plant, with those close to the ground being hori-

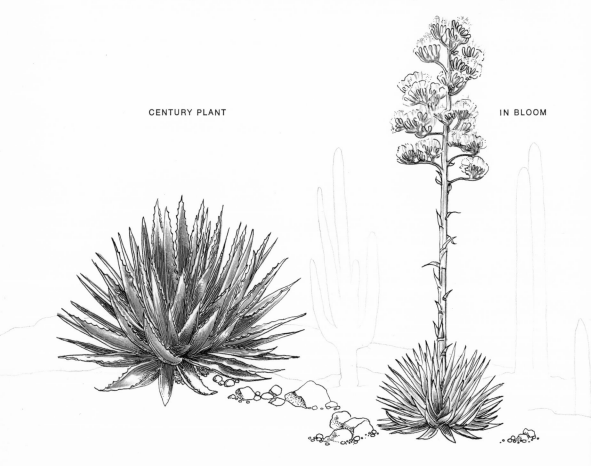

CENTURY PLANT

IN BLOOM

zontal and graduating to vertical in the center. If the sharp outermost points on these leaves were covered with a blanket the effect would be of a domed half ball.

After attaining full growth in a few years, development seems to cease as far as plant enlargement is concerned. However, five, ten, or twenty years later there is a gradual thickening of each leaf and then, from the exact center, a stalk commences to take on the shape of a six-inch-thick asparagus spear, rising straight toward the sky. At this time, the century plant becomes active and in a few months the stalk attains a height of thirty or more feet. Its elongation, which is sometimes as great as eight inches per day, can almost be seen in its upward movement. Then the flowers open at the top in one of the most beautiful floral displays to be seen on the desert. By this time, the leaves at the base of the stalk are wrinkled and brown—having expended their years of stored energy in one last glorious moment of splendor.

The conservation of a moisture-derived energy reaches its peak

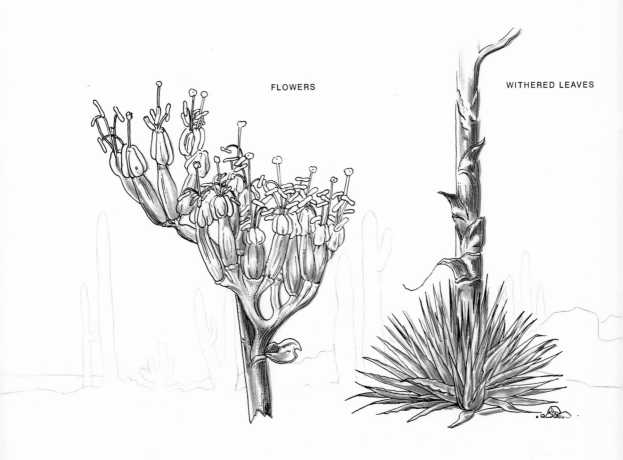

FLOWERS

WITHERED LEAVES

in a strange tuberous plant called the Ibervilla which lives on some of the arid islands in the Gulf of California. Year after year the clue of its presence on the surface is a rounded knob which so closely resembles nearby rocks that its existence is rarely detected. But when a chubasco comes up from the south to dump its torrential rains, there is a sudden awakening in the plant from years of dormancy. Sinuous vinelike branches almost immediately cover the ground, bloom for a few days and then wither and die, permitting the tremendous bulb beneath to return to its deathlike slumber.

In all desert life the conservation of water is of prime importance but an experience with a fifty-pound bulb of the Ibervilla at the Arizona-Sonora Desert Museum shows that this plant has developed the trait far beyond that of most others. One of these bulbs, removed from Catalina Island, was placed on the high shelf of a storeroom and forgotten for at least ten years. When discovered a decade later, shrunken and seemingly dead, it was tossed on a dump. A week passed and then a July rain deluged the area, triggering the "dead" plant to action by causing it to spread its vines over the surrounding area.

Chapter 3

The Sturdy Cacti

And the desert becomes alive in an interminable chain made up of various links from lichens to annuals to perennials. But the most spectacular and specialized of all the plants that have achieved success in the botanical world of the desert community is the cactus. The exact origin of this family is largely a matter of conjecture but most botanists believe that the ancient forebear was similar to a rose plant which still exists in Central America. No matter what the ancestors were, it is safe to say that cactus as a family has utilized every specialty developed by other plants that have survived in the desert.

The hundreds of species that make up the cactus family vary from peanut size to giants that tower almost fifty feet into the air and weigh up to eight tons. Although there are none that survive on an annual basis (living for but one year and producing seeds from which come next year's plants), there are a few that are rather short-lived. They reproduce by means of sucker plants that spring from the roots of the parent plant prior to its death.

IBERVILLA

By contrast there are others which may reach an age of from two hundred to three hundred years.

If we were to make some comparisons, the bulbous root of the Ibervilla could well be matched with that of the cactus known as the night-blooming cereus. Throughout most of each year, the only parts of the cereus showing aboveground are four or five branching stems, gray-green in color and rarely in excess of one-half inch in thickness. We know that they are more delicate than most of the cactus family because of their placement on the desert. They are rarely found in the open, usually surviving only under the protective branches of desert shrubs or trees. Beneath the unobtrusive stems is the main part of the plant—a tremendous bulb hidden from sight by a shallow ground covering.

From June 30 to June 1 of the following year the plant is inactive. It does not seem to grow—even its straggly stems are reluctant to sway in a breeze. But somewhere in this comatose plant there is a timer that controls the blooming of the cereus. The timer signals to the individual plant when it is to commence budding. For several weeks the buds elongate until they reach a length of about three inches. Then, on only one night a year, the plant bursts forth into bloom. Dusk brings a slight separation of the flower sheaths and when darkness envelops the country-side the gleaming cream-white petals unfold with a blooming action so rapid that a human eye can detect the motion. An hour later many of the four-inch blooms peek from under the protective bushes and trees and attract the night-flying insects by exuding one of the most pleasing aromas ever released by any flower.

After that single night when insects fertilize the plants the petals rapidly wither. Morning finds them drooped and ugly. However, in the weeks that follow, a gleaming red seed pod at the base of each withered flower appears. Its size, design, and coloring are—like the aroma of the blooms—obviously meant to attract attention. Within a few days after ripening most of the pods will be carried underground by small rodents, where a few of the seeds will germinate and the cycle will start over again.

The night-blooming cereus, although it is a member of the family which is best known for its spines, is almost devoid of them, having just occasional sharpened bumps neither ornamental nor protective. It may have been that the plant had real spines long ago, but because they were painful when touched, they thwarted the allure of the red fruits. Probably the spineless members of the species dominated. Of course this is just wild conjecture; no one knows for sure—but the spines of cacti, like the creosote taste of the greasewood bush, supposedly keep the otherwise edible plants from being used either as food or liquid. The cereus carries its moisture underground, and its skinny stems, reinforced with a woody fiber, are not very tasty.

The various species of the barrel cactus, however, have an entirely different texture, a pulpy body which can be described best as of a soft watermelon consistency. On these heavy-bodied plants the spines are very efficient, for each one measures a good two inches in length and is not only rigidly anchored but also has its outer end sharpened and abruptly recurved. A thirsty mammal might force its nose into this maze of hooks undamaged, but in removing it, would suffer pain and lacerations.

The barrel cactus, minus its protective spines, is a food for many animals. This is readily shown by its use in Lower California during years of drought. Some parts of this peninsula receive less than two inches of rainfall per year, barely enough to sustain life. Let the rainfall drop a fraction below normal and all the living things suffer. Cattle, creatures bred to a state of human dependency, are the hardest hit and the first to die. The Mexican cowboys prevent some deaths, however, by burning the spines from the barrels and then, with machetes, exposing the moisture-storing pulp within. As a temporary lifesaver, barrel cacti have also been used by human beings who have become stranded on a desert. If the top of the plant is sheared off, the internal pulp pounded with a stick, squeezed, and removed, some of the thirst-quenching liquid will collect in the bottom.

46

BARREL CACTUS

As far as it is known, however, no one has ever praised the flavor.

Most, if not all, plants have phototropic tendencies which draw them toward the sun to reap the benefits from its energy-releasing rays. The blooms of some, such as sunflowers, actually follow the sun's arc from dawn to dusk. Most cacti are rigid and unbending, so if phototropic tendencies exist they are so minor that they remain unnoticed. However, the barrel is such an exception that it bears the name "compass plant" in some regions. Its massive columnar bodies rarely grow in a vertical position. Most lean perceptibly toward the southwest.

In contrast to the massive spines of the barrel, there are the infinitesimal ones found on the beavertail. These are so small that they are almost dustlike in appearance, so different from the usual that botanists call them by the strange name of "glochids" which, in Greek derivation, means "point of an arrow" and in botanical circles "barbed as a hair." Frankly, if hairs were barbed as are beavertail glochids, baldness would be a blessing. Due to their tiny size they are one of the meanest of all cactus spines. They dig into the skin with a vengeance and are so small that they are very hard to remove and it is difficult to relieve the itching pain.

Despite the glochids, however, beavertails in bloom are some of the most beautiful of all cacti. The flattened segments, from four to eight inches across, are a gray-green color evenly spotted with brown bumps of spines. On the edge of each pad (the beaver tails from which the plant gets its name) the spectacular three-inch blooms burst forth. Each petal is more delicate than those found on the most delicate rose ever produced, blending reds, yellows, purples, and blues that words can never adequately portray.

All but a few of the hundreds of species of cacti are capable of rooting from a cutting, or from a part of the plant that has fallen to the ground. One species in the group of chollas, known as the "jumping cactus," has developed this trait to such an extent that the plant is now incapable of producing living seeds.

It still goes through the motions of seed production, such as blossoming in the spring of the year to be fertilized by insects. Seeds commence to develop; but then the action ceases. Instead of ripening, the four- or five-inch segments of the plant, upon which the blossoms appeared, droop downward and their anchorage to supporting stems becomes so weak that they will fall apart at the slightest touch.

It is from this fragility of the outermost branches that the plant has falsely gained the name of "jumping cactus." In actuality, the plant does not jump; instead, when an animal inadvertently brushes by, the slightest touch will make a barbed spine dig into the animal with such a grip that the entire drooping segment will break loose. This in turn permits other spines to take hold and in what seems like a single action the plant has jumped aboard to hitch a ride to distant areas.

Chollas, being treelike cacti, have internal woody supports which run up the main trunks and to the branches. When the plant is alive, these supports are coated with the characteristic green pulp and then liberally covered with spines. At death, however, these coverings are lost, but the gaunt skeletons are so well suited for stresses and strains that a structural engineer would be justly proud of creating the design. This wood reinforcement is not so solid as it is in trees from other life zones, but it is tubular—eliminating excess weight—and then, in a further effort toward lightness, the tubes are riddled with holes.

After the death of one of these well-stressed chollas, the hot sun beating down upon them bleaches the dry wood while fierce desert winds carrying sand polish off the rough edges. When so conditioned by the elements they become sought-after objects for gadget furniture manufacturers and have reached the far corners of the world, in the form of lamp stands, book ends, or other ornamental creations.

Cacti have been used by man for centuries. Parts of the plant have probably been utilized from the time that man first immigrated to this continent to become an integral part of the desert ecology. Indian legends point to many medicinal properties. We do not know, however, whether most were really effective or just mental treatments for psychosomatic ailments. However, at the present time, derivatives from the pads of prickly pears are used in treating diabetes and as stimulants for certain types of heart trouble.

Markets in southern Mexico sell the young pads of the prickly pear as "nopalitos" and the fruits of these same plants form the basic flavoring for some jellies, syrups, and candies. Until about a decade ago there was a commercial venture in the raising of prickly pears in southern California for market distribution. At that time the fruits had mainly a novelty value but as the human population becomes more numerous—who can tell what we may be eating in the future? Prickly pears may sometime come back as a regular part of our diet.

There is no doubt that mankind will find other uses for the

cactus in the future, even beyond its utilization as a food for human beings. At the present time liquid from crushed prickly-pear pads is becoming increasingly popular for the removal of rust and chemical scale from boiler tubes. Seeds from fruits of the barrel cactus were at one time collected and sold as chicken feed, and in the early part of this century Luther Burbank succeeded in crossing varieties to produce a spineless creation. If pruned correctly, this hybrid retains its spineless character and is used as an emergency food for cattle.

Cactus had an important place in the founding of the chain of missions along the coast of Lower California and Upper California. There are still almost spineless varieties growing at mission ruins. A few of these ruins still have square cleared areas of an acre or more that are completely fenced with patayha cactus, a thick-stemmed heavily armored species that grows into an impassable tangled maze up to six feet high. In such a corral, hoofed animals could never escape.

One of the strangest human uses of one of the cacti concerns peyote, a small insignificant plant which protrudes but a mere three inches above the soils of northern Mexico. Just when it was discovered that the eating of this plant caused extraordinary color perception is lost to the unwritten past, but the chances are that some Indian, possibly pre-Aztec, chewed and swallowed one purely for the moisture it contained. Perhaps after a short rest, as he was awaiting darkness to return to camp, he awoke deathly sick—but between retchings his world became one of vivid color in a series of hallucinations that lasted for many hours. News of his experience might have spread from tribe to tribe and by the time the Spaniards arrived in Mexico the peyote had divine connotations, providing a short cut to the world of the gods.

Even its collection took on ritual procedures, for on starting a journey to the areas where it grew, sacred verses, incantations, and prayers filled the air. Before each plant was picked from the soil the Indian offered penance to his native gods. If there were devout converts to Christianity among them they might cross themselves in the name of the Father, the Son, and the Holy Spirit.

Throughout the centuries of the use of peyote by primitive Indians, its true characteristics remained hidden in the dogmas of their religions. Returning missionaries saw in its use what they wanted to see and not necessarily what was scientifically correct in regard to its effect on the human body. Some saw it as a simple addition to the sacrificial bread and wine rites used by many churches. Others claimed that its use furthered debauchery and that the halo of veneration placed upon it hindered their efforts toward the conversion of the "savages."

Late in the nineteenth century, however, scientists around the world became interested in all the drug-producing plants and various experiments were made. Some of them have resulted in the wonder drugs that are benefiting mankind today. Non-superstitious researchers became the guinea pigs. Here are a few quotes from some of their notes while under the influence of peyote.

"Stars, delicate floating films of color, then an abrupt rush of countless points of white lights swept across the field of vision, as if the unseen millions of the Milky Way were to flow in a sparkling river."

"All the colors ever beheld are dull in comparison to these."

"They still linger visibly in memory and left the feeling that seen among them were colors unknown."

Havelock Ellis wrote of his experiences, "Then the pictures became more definite, but too confused and crowded to be described beyond saying that they were of the same character of the images of the kaleidoscope, symmetrical groupings of spiked objects."

In the writings about the effect of mescaline, the ingredient in peyote that causes these color hallucinations, a few of the researchers mention delightful odors and a distinctive warming of all surface skin. All of them mention severe nausea soon after the cactus is eaten but practically no aftereffects when the "show" has ended. Strangely, throughout these sensations and visions, the mind of the researcher not only continues to function but acquires an increased lucidity. It appears that claims of mescaline addiction are completely unfounded. Currently this insignificant cactus is simply bolstering the superstitions of Indians, or is the plaything, along with LSD and marijuana, of amateur experimenters. If, in the future, medical science devises some way to utilize its fantastic properties in the treatment of psychotic ailments it could become the most important cactus known. Until that day, however, the giant saguaro deserves the honor.

SAGUARO BLOSSOMS AND BUDS

Chapter 4

The Monarch of the Desert Plants

The naming of the saguaro as the state plant of Arizona was not recognition without due cause. Throughout man's entire association with the plant, even back to prehistoric days, the saguaro's presence has made life a little easier. In each life zone of the world there seems to be one of these all-important plants to mankind. In the tropics it's the Manihot, supplier of starch foods to the natives (tapioca to us); on the islands of the Pacific it would be the cocoanut; on the deserts of Africa the date palm; and on the Arizona deserts it is definitely the saguaro.

The saguaro, most majestic of cacti, at the start of its life is a weakling with a slow growth. A small number, if any, of its seeds would germinate and survive were it not for the protection and help that they get from the desert plants and animals which together create the desert community.

Imagine a full-sized saguaro, one that has already attained an age of at least a century and a half, a weight of about four tons, and a height of approximately thirty-five feet. Three or four arms branch from its main trunk and, in July, every arm as well as the main trunk, is crowned with a halo of brilliant red fruits. Each of these fruits contains about four thousand seeds, bringing the number of possible offspring in seed form to almost a million. All of these come from a single plant and all are the product of a single season. But there are periods of ten, twenty, or thirty years when not a single one of these many "possibles" finds conditions just right for successful germination.

As an example of these constant seasonal failures, let's take a quick look at the ten acres of fenced area which comprises Tucson's Arizona-Sonora Desert Museum. Within its ten acres there are between one hundred and fifty to two hundred saguaros, with the oldest probably in the neighborhood of two hundred years and the youngest ten to fifteen years of age.

These adult plants scatter many millions of seeds each year, and one would suppose that within the fenced area plants could be found with an even gradation from young to aged. Such is not the case, however, for in the juvenile bracket there are only about a dozen that stand about three feet tall. Their estimated age would be somewhere around fifteen years. The next size rises to about twelve feet. There are about twenty of these and their estimated age is around forty-five years. Next are the twenty-footers which are quite common. Their age has been guessed at about seventy-five years. And then there are the big ones of about thirty to thirty-five feet that have lived for close to a century and a half. But between these distinctive age brackets there are almost no intermediate sizes, showing that a whole chain of exacting requirements must be co-ordinated before any saguaro seed can achieve successful growth.

Weather is probably the main growth factor, but even in ideal weather, germination would fail but for the actions of the entire ecological community, a community of other plants that have enriched the soil through the centuries, plants that afford shade to a newborn seedling and protect it from cold during winter months. Birds also do their share, for in feeding on the

56

tasty fruits, they carry some seeds to favorite roosts where the seeds drop to the ground. There they are picked up by hungry rodents. Many are eaten but a few reach underground storage chambers. If burrowing insects have aerated the soil, not too much and not too little, but just the right amount, then moisture from the summer rains may start the seed's germination.

Thousands of seeds probably get this far, but on germinating and breaking the ground surface, most of the infant plants emerge into a forbidding world where they are either destroyed by the rays of the fierce sun beating upon them or trampled by the sharp hooves of peccary or deer. If the population of hawks, coyotes, and shunks is low, then the rodent population will be high and the seedlings will become food for them. And conversely, if when the seeds were dropped by the birds the year before, rodents were scarce due to predators being abundant, then many would not have been planted at all.

Even if the multitude of terrestrial conditions is delicately balanced, storms may enter the picture. Too much rain can rot the young plants; too little can desiccate them. Too many clouds can chill them; too few can have the opposite effect. To make a long story short, the survival of an infant saguaro is based on an interminable series of "ifs" and could well be compared to the opening of a complicated safe. Miss just one of a long series of numbers, or turn the dial just a fraction in the wrong direction, and their door to life will fail to open. It is only once in every twenty years or so that all the forces of nature hit the right combination.

When one of the millions of otherwise wasted seeds germinates, the tiny black object little larger than the head of a pin simultaneously forces roots into the ground and breaks the surface soil with a fuzzy growth the size of a honeybee. That fragile life, barely above the ground, carries on photosynthesis, permitting a taproot to grow and form an anchorage. This underground part grows downward with four or five times the speed of the young saguaro above. After several years its length might stretch

to more than a foot, firmly anchoring the seemingly stunted cactus above. Now, although it has enlarged only a little, the cactus has successfully passed the infant stage.

The plant's growth becomes more evenly divided, some above and some below, but now the subterranean effort switches to laterals—tiny rootlets just under the surface that run out horizontally in all directions. At an age of about ten to fifteen years the growth of the cactus has reached two or maybe three feet, but the laterals—like the radiating spokes of a wheel—have spread to encompass a circle about a dozen feet across. With this intercepting network, each rain, no matter how little it permeates the soil, will be sucked in and transported for storage in the complicated young plant above.

The complications are many, running from the tip ends of

the thorny protective coating to the exact center of the cylindrical growth, each having a life or death bearing on each other until combined they form a workable mechanism that could last for several centuries. Among the many factors that permit survival, there must be a timer that signals the plant to change spine design when a certain growth is achieved. This mechanism can be likened to a boy's change of voice or his growth of whiskers when he passes puberty. On the saguaro, in its growth to five or six feet, the spines are rigid and sharp, all pointing in a general downward direction—a discouraging arrangement to any climbing animal. Later in life, however, the character of the spines changes, never to the point of becoming an inviting freeway, but limber enough to permit passage by a hungry rodent who might help the saguaro by spreading its seeds.

Even as seedlings, the plants show a lengthwise fluted arrangement like the ribs of a half-closed accordion. These serve in several capacities for they not only hold the spines on their outermost ridges, but like the spines, they may give a slight bit more shade than would be available to a perfectly smooth cylindrical plant. Their main function, however, is their flexibility, which permits a swelling or contraction like an accordion, depending on the changes of weather. In the cactus it is water, most precious of all elements, that is held in suspension, causing pressure. This pressure is the force that causes expansion and contraction.

When the saguaro reaches its maximum height (forty-nine feet seems to be a record), its radiating spokelike roots grow on all sides to a distance of seventy-five feet or more. Their placement just under the surface permits them to receive a rapid signal that rainfall is occurring and in a very short time smaller rootlets emerge, permitting the transportation of water to the massive parent plant. This is evenly transported from top to bottom and after certain chemical changes have taken place it is stored for future use in the fibrous tissue.

It is in this storage that the fluted skin of the cactus shows its remarkable versatility. All during the previous months of drought there is shrinkage; grooves become smaller and ridges closer together. If, just before a rain, a belt is loosely draped around a saguaro and then checked a day or so after a downpour—the looseness will not only have vanished but the belt will have cut into the expanding plant. Circumference may increase as much as five inches, not just where the belt was placed but all the way up the trunk which, with the swelling, is rapidly gaining a more cylindrical shape. Imagine the amount of water necessary for such a feat. Some authorities have estimated that a cactus may absorb and store aboveground over two tons in a single storm.

This in itself is fantastic but even more so is the ability of the plant to bear the weight, for well over 75 per cent of its material is of a soft watermelon consistency. Through its center, however, there are a dozen or more rounded strips of a woody fiber with interlocking connections one to the other. On a twenty-foot plant with a twelve-inch diameter they would occupy only about one-twentieth of its sectional bulk, so none is more

CROSS SECTION OF SAGUARO STEM

than an inch in diameter. If they had the rigidity of hardwood, such as oak, strength could be assumed, but these internal sticks are damp and flexible and when dry are brittle. The secret is a complicated system of harnessed stresses which could well have been used by the early aeronautical designers in their quest for lightweight and extreme support.

The support that this seemingly weak internal bracing gives to the saguaro could easily be understood if all the pressure were directed downward. However, many of the plants, instead of being straight columns, have tons of branches protruding from the sides. This could still be understood if the branches balanced each other in a type of symmetry, with equal weight on all sides of this column. But cacti are so lopsided with branches on only one side that the uneven weight should make them topple. The plant seemingly survives by a peculiar brute strength, miraculously held aloft by a series of fragile ribs. Singly, any one of them can be broken with ease. The immortal words: "United we stand, divided we fall" could well be applied to this wonderful plant.

These ribs of the saguaro, like parts of other cacti, have always been used by man. On the desert where almost every plant has stickers of one sort or another, the smooth saguaro ribs had been in great demand. Until about a century ago the Papago Indians who lived in saguaro country inhabited igloo-shaped houses made largely of sacaton grasses, saguaro ribs, and other material that could be harvested nearby. Long flexible poles were a necessity for they could be bent and tied with leather thongs into the latticed shape of a half dome, six or eight feet high and about a dozen feet across.

After these smooth saguaro ribs were lashed rigidly in place, forming a foundation, branches with long thorns every half inch or so were stripped from ocotillo and laid over the top. Then grass was brought in and applied upside down starting at ground level. Each successive tier overlapped the one below in a shingling that finally covered the original framework of saguaro ribs and ocotillo branches. From within a finished grass house tiny

62

bits of sky could be seen through many cracks. Strangely, however, leakage rarely occurred because water dripping on the sloping grass ran to its end, then dropped to another tier, and eventually reached the ground while the inside remained dry.

Although such houses were very primitive by our standards, they were admirably adapted for desert living, supplying shade without cutting off breezes that filtered through the loose grasses. When these grass houses were doused with water on a scorching summer day, temperatures within would drop many degrees. Some of the containers used by the Papagos for applying the water were of saguaro origin, being formed by the plant's sap hardening into durable gourds around woodpecker holes.

The saguaro's greatest importance to the earliest desert peoples, however, was the food that the plant supplied. So important were its summer fruits to Indian economy that the collection of them in late spring and summer was almost a religious ritual. Even the simple act of hooking them from the tip ends of the arms, with long saguaro ribs, had to be done in a prescribed way; and when the fruits were laid on the ground it was always with open side up. If reversed, the people believed that rain would not bless the country. Another indication of the plant's importance was that its fruiting season signaled the start of a new year, so in a way, the lives of the Papagos pivoted on an all-important date set by this cactus.

The Papago's greatest festival was known by the name of "navaita," a word derived from "navait," the red wine of the saguaro fruit. In ancient days this was more than just an intoxicating beverage. When the fruits were brought to camp after harvest they were first boiled down into a syrup. This served a double purpose, for by concentrating the sugar content, preservation was achieved. The boiling also separated the tiny black seeds from the pulp. These seeds were later crushed and made into flour.

Most of the syrup was used as food, but some was reserved for Papago medicine men in the making of their red wine. Their fermentation system was simple, consisting of the addition of

about four parts of water and then storing the brew in a grass hut where there was considerable warmth. At the festival honoring the saguaro, some of the wine was used as a sacrifice and finger-flicked toward the four corners of the earth as appeasement or thanks to the Papago gods.

Another indication of early man's reverence for the saguaro was shown by their extreme care of the plant. The giant cactus was disturbed only for its fruits or, after a plant had already died from natural causes, for its materials. The other plants on the desert had no such protection.

If present-day Papagos still had these same taboos, our methods of clearing land could cause an Indian war. On the outskirts of some cities in the Southwest, bulldozers work around the clock knocking down these venerable giants to clear an area for a housing development. Then after the homes are constructed the householders expensively struggle to transport a few new saguaros to take the place of those destroyed. They might, with luck, get some of the plants back; but how about the birds, the lizards, and the small mammals that at some seasons depend upon saguaros for a livelihood? Throughout the rest of the year their diet consists of noxious insects, scorpions, centipedes, and unwanted weed seeds. Once that delicate balance is destroyed it is difficult to restore on manicured land.

But what of the saguaro in the over-all scheme of things? What is its ecology in regard to the lower forms of life that also must survive in the desert's wild kingdom?

About one out of every three mature saguaros will have brownish abrasions. If these are found close to the ground they are probably the result of a bruise such as from a thrown rock. But if the abrasions are high on the trunk and appear as round holes, they could be the homes of any one of a dozen species of feathered desert dwellers, dependent on saguaros for nesting sites. Only two of these, the Gila woodpecker and the flicker, have the ability to excavate nest holes in the cactus. All the rest of the cavity-nesting birds use the woodpeckers' deserted nests after they have been occupied for a season or more.

66

GILA WOODPECKER

GILDED FLICKER

ELF OWL AND NEST

The whole procedure sounds simple. A woodpecker wants to drill a hole, so it goes to the saguaro of its choice and starts to work. The soft texture of the plant makes labor easy and after going in horizontally for five or six inches, it turns the tunnel downward and excavates a roomy chamber about the size of a small loaf of bread. In the bottom of this chamber the bird will lay its eggs which will hatch after incubation. The young grow in size, leave the chamber, and start drilling their own holes. This simple method of nesting really has many unthought-of complications. Any one of them can mean the difference between life and death. The survival of the plant hangs on a few fragile threads and the one of primary importance is weather and its rainfall.

The saguaro belt, which stretches across southern Arizona, has two distinct seasons when the skies become overcast and precipitation occurs. The winter storms, usually starting at the end of the year, are rarely violent and cease in February. The summer storms, accompanied by lightning, thunder, and flash floods, start the first or second week in July and continue spasmodically until the middle of September. During both of these wet seasons the saguaros absorb the surface water and are perceptibly swollen until losses during the dry times thin them down. Before this thinning process occurs there is internal pressure when the liquids within have not yet attained the normal sap viscosity. For the cactus these are periods of extreme danger, periods when bruises or cuts can cause the death of century-old giants.

In most areas of the world where woodpeckers live they chisel on woody trees at any season, but the two that live in association with saguaros seem to have an instinctive knowledge of "when" or "when not" to work. They usually time their home building to the short period when the sap has thickened to the point where it can scab over any wounds before irreparable damage is done. This healing process of the cactus might be likened to the successive coats exuded by an oyster in coating a pearl. The saguaros, however, do their coating on the inside of a cavity and not around the outside of an irritating object, as is done within the shellfish.

As the woodpecker digs his way in, there is a flow of the thickened sap down the ever-deepening walls. Within the day or so that it takes to finish the desired chamber, the entrance tunnel will have already started to harden into a material akin to the lightweight lacquer trays of the Orient. Within another few days the entire cavity has a paper-thin coating, insulating the drying air from pulling moisture out of the plant.

From then on layers are added until, after several years, a quarter-inch shell results. The strength of this creation is so astounding that it can withstand the pressure of a saguaro's shrinkage and thus cause a visible bump on the plant at the location of a bird's nest. Its durability is so great that fifty or a hundred years later the giant can fall and be absorbed back into the soil with the only clue of past existence, the shoelike gourds that were formed to heal a wound.

During the short season when the healing abilities of saguaros are at their peak, the Gila woodpeckers and flickers are industrious, but they often build homes that are not satisfactory. So they build others. As a result of their industriousness, there is no shortage of cavities, a situation which makes life on the desert possible for other bird species which otherwise would be forced to seek homes in distant areas and thus remove from the desert a most important link in its ecological chain.

The loss of any single bird species could be disastrous. For example, the woodpeckers seem to be the primary key which makes the occupation of so many other animals a possibility. There is hardly a plant on the desert that at one time or another is not attacked by bark-boring insects. In limited numbers their depredations are negligible and possibly a necessary evil. Unchecked, however, they could destroy the plants on which they live. Woodpeckers eliminate many of these internal parasites for when the birds are not engaged in their short period of nest building, they constantly search the desert and its plants for insect food.

After the woodpeckers have vacated their nests, the small predatory birds move in. The three best-known are the diurnal sparrow hawk, the nocturnal elf, and the screech owl. Of these, the sparrow hawks are the only ones patrolling the desert during the day. The owls do similar work at night. If small rodents increase beyond their normal abundance or beyond what is good for the desert community, then these small predators center their attention on them. After the rodents are reduced, it might be some injurious insect that the birds focus their talents upon.

Another group whose residence is also dependent on saguaros is working the airways above. This "patrol" consists of several species of flycatchers and colonies of purple martins. The flycatchers work fairly close to the ground and as their name implies feed on the multitude of insects which have air-borne transportation. The martins, however, patrol the air high above the tallest saguaros and eat migratory insects.

It might seem that the killing of a few bugs or moths or rodents has no great bearing on the over-all welfare of the desert, but plants are subject to disease as are all animate creatures. And—just as diseases are carried to animals and human beings by insects they are also carried to plants, sometimes with deadly results. As an illustration of how a slight upset of nature's scheme can ruin the interrelationship of insects, birds, and saguaros, consider a study made at Tucson's botanical laboratories a few years ago.

As human occupation of the desert lands increased, it was noticed that many of the saguaros along roadways were dying from a peculiar disease. The first sign of the disease was a brownish cast surrounding bruises or cuts that had been made by thoughtless people. This was followed by the seepage of a tarlike substance from a constantly enlarging area. Within a few months a plant that took a century or more to grow would become a wasted skeleton.

Research showed that this was caused by a bacterial infection which could not spread its damage unaided. It had to be carried by something and subsequent studies disclosed the fact that a moth was the carrier. On an unbruised cactus this insect had to spend time penetrating the waxy plant covering, which gave the birds a chance to eliminate the culprit before the infection was implanted. On an injured plant, however, the contamination from the moth was almost instantaneous.

There is no doubt that woodpeckers cause the death of some saguaros. However, in their work they make nesting and residence possible for a host of birds which save many more cacti than woodpeckers ever destroy. This nesting of other birds is due to a variety of factors such as the shade cast by spines and longitudinal ridges, the waxy coating which reflects light before it is transformed into heat, and the moisture-filled bulk of the plant. Two or three tons of liquid, especially when protected by the insulating skin of the cactus, are slow to rise in temperature and also slow to drop in temperature.

The saguaro with a nest hole has a mean internal temperature of eighty degrees when the eastern sky glows with the rays of a rising sun. By the time the sun has covered one-quarter of its arc across the sky the air temperature will have risen to ninety or ninety-five degrees, while the interior of the cactus will jump only a degree or two. Thermometers, just after midday, will hit about 105 degrees but the internal parts of the cactus will barely reach eighty-seven degrees. Then a general lowering occurs. Soon after dark temperatures will balance, both at about eighty-five degrees; but by midnight the air may plunge to a chilly seventy degrees, which would be at least ten degrees lower than the plant with its built-in regulator.

This leveling of temperatures may not seem overly important at first glance. However, if the peculiar exacting requirements necessary for the hatching of eggs is understood it will then be seen to be a condition which not only offers comfort to the birds but is almost imperative for successful incubation. When an egg is first laid the spark of life is dormant and will remain so for several days unless temperatures rise to the nineties. If this should occur, life begins and from then on the egg becomes a delicate mechanism with survival being dependent on controlled warmth that is maintained two or three degrees on either side of one hundred. A drop lasting several hours below that narrow span will kill it, and conversely a rise above it, even a slight one, can cause deformities in the chick that will emerge.

In addition to this heat requirement there is also a humidity requirement, based upon the maintenance of moisture in relation to temperature. Birds have various ways to control these necessities. Their normal body heat hovers in the vicinity of 103 degrees, so by sitting close on the eggs this optimum warmth is transferred to them. If outside heat is too great they are capable of creating a slight cooling effect by shading, and possibly by releasing enough moisture to have evaporation do the job.

On the Salton Sea where temperatures often climb to 120 degrees, the nesting white pelicans make constant trips to the shores of their small island and return to the eggs with breast feathers dripping. Body release of moisture, and the dripping feathers of the pelicans also, help to control the humidity. Within the saguaros, however, well over half of this battle is already won.

So there is a balance. The birds eat insect pests, and the plants make possible a residence in an otherwise uninviting land.

There can be no doubt that the abundance of flowers and fruits of saguaros also invite other birds. The white-winged doves, for instance, make their United States visitations within the period of the emergence of the first flower buds and the drop-off of the last fruits. If unusual weather conditions make the buds appear earlier than customary the doves seem to leave their wintering grounds in Mexico a little earlier. And although they usually depart about September 1, if, by chance, winds in mid-August cause the fruits to drop—the doves advance their date of fall migration accordingly. It is almost like clockwork, with food in the offing, or food disappearing, as the deciding factor.

The majority of desert flowers are cross-fertilized by insects such as beetles, moths, wasps, and bees, but recent studies made

73

DOVE VISITATION

by University of Arizona students have shown that a species of pollen-eating bats is important to saguaros. These highly specialized flying mammals have approximately the same migratory urge as that of the whitewing dove. They leave their winter homes in Mexican caves a little later than the birds and arrive in the Tucson area when the earliest of the saguaro blooms commence to appear. During daylight hours they hang on the ceiling of a special chamber in Colossal Cave, emerging after dark to feed on saguaro pollen by poking their long tongues and pointed noses deep into the stamens of the flowers. Most, if not all, of this bat species that extends its range north to Arizona, are females which bear and raise their young with us before retreating to rejoin associates in warmer climates.

Chapter 5

Interdependence of Life

There is mystery on the desert. The time to look for it is in the early morning when the rising sun has just breached the eastern horizon to cast long shadows on the ground. The place to look is any one of the sand dunes where the quirks of winds move sand back and forth with such frequency that the face

of the country changes from day to day. To the casual observer
the rolling dunes might appear to be dead, but close scrutiny
of the ground will show entrancing fleeting patterns of tiny tracks
left by the life that roamed under cover of darkness. It's the
"sandscript" of a few arachnids—spiders and their relatives—and
of countless insects.

That such an area could support life of any kind seems incongruous for throughout most of the year the dunes are the
epitome of barrenness. But looks are deceiving; let a single rain
get off course to douse the region and the dormant seeds of
annuals awaken to spread a carpet of blooms in their short-lived
moment of glory. Drying winds soon ruin the stability that the
dampness has given the tiny grains of soil, and with the sand
on the move some of the plants are sand-blasted to oblivion.
Others on the sides of the rises are buried under tons of wind-
blown materials that with aridity start their aimless migrations
once more.

With separation of the dustlike particles the creatures that
roam at night again leave a written record of their travels. And
some, if the hour is early and the temperature low, might still
be abroad. Let's follow one of the more common tracks to see
where it will lead, and perhaps if luck is with us—learn the
identity of the creature that made these etchings in the sands

at our feet. The track is about an inch wide, consisting of two parallel lines with a half-inch space in the center, undisturbed. Each of these lines has tiny indentations across its width which look for all the world like the treads of a caterpillar tractor in extreme miniature.

As this track progresses over the rolling sand dunes, the horizontal areas show its print in minute detail; but on upward slopes there is skidding—on down grades, a sliding. At one spot another similar trail almost intercepts and then abruptly turns off. Six or eight inches before the near collision, however, there is a marked change in the imprints. Both show a furrow in the center areas that were previously clear. This should have been our clue to identity but we passed it by. And, had our nostrils been close to the ground and as sensitized as the noses of some animals—another clue would have been detected at the spot.

Fifty feet farther on, the track-maker was still plodding along and we discovered that it was a beetle. But when we approached to within a yard of him, ground vibrations or air-carried sound tipped him off to our presence and the black beetle's body tilted to a vertical position. His pointed rear was lifted a full inch and a half from the ground and his mouth parts submerged in the sand between his front feet. After our moment of motionless observation he started forward once more, not hurrying, but for a few inches seemingly forgetting to resume his horizontal traveling position. In that short space his tracks showed the nose print that were seen back on the trail when the two pinacate beetles converged on their collision course.

Here was a survival technique, one not based on deceptive form, color, or speed, but instead on a tiny stream or spray of evil-smelling fluid emitted from the pointed tail. That it is efficacious in saving the life of this insect is proven by their abundance—an abundance so great that a fabulous land of volcanic craters on the Mexican side of the border is known as the "Pinacates." The vinegaroon, a harmless arachnid, related to the spider, and the rainworm, a many legged caterpillar-like creature, that appear in multitudes in July, use other repellent odors in the same way. The vinegaroon, as the name implies, has a stale vinegar smell that lingers for hours, while the rainworm's odor is that of hydrocyanic acid which can kill if inhaled in excess.

By midmorning the gentle breezes that began playing over the dunes when the sun rose will have erased the fragile insect script that was left on the sand from the night before. The beetles, the caterpillars, the spiders, and other arachnids that nightly make their temporary highways, will have retreated to a cooler underground world. Temperature studies have been made on many of our western deserts and they all prove that sand is a wonderful insulator despite the fact that the closer a person approaches sunlit sand the hotter the temperature becomes. To average the results of these studies we can do an experiment. If the air temperature of 125 degrees exists in the shade at the height of a standing man's face, and if we lower the thermometer to one foot aboveground, we will find the temperature hovering around 150 degrees. At one inch aboveground it will be over 160 degrees, and on the actual surface about 180 degrees.

Now let's go underground with the thermometer to see why many animals do so during hours of daylight. The 180 degrees will penetrate for a few inches, but at a depth of five or six inches it will have dropped to that which exists at the height of the standing man's face. At ten inches below surface it will be ninety or ninety-five degrees, and at a foot and a half it will be a pleasant eighty degrees. Some might not consider eighty degrees comfortable, but here comparison enters the picture. Remember the tests in school where three pans of water were placed on a table? The first had a few ice cubes, the second was air temperature, and the third lukewarm. A hand immersed in the first and then momentarily placed in the second felt warmth or heat. A hand placed in the third and then in the second seemed cold. Imagine the difference a creature must feel between the 180 degrees surface temperature and the greatly lowered one existing just one foot below!

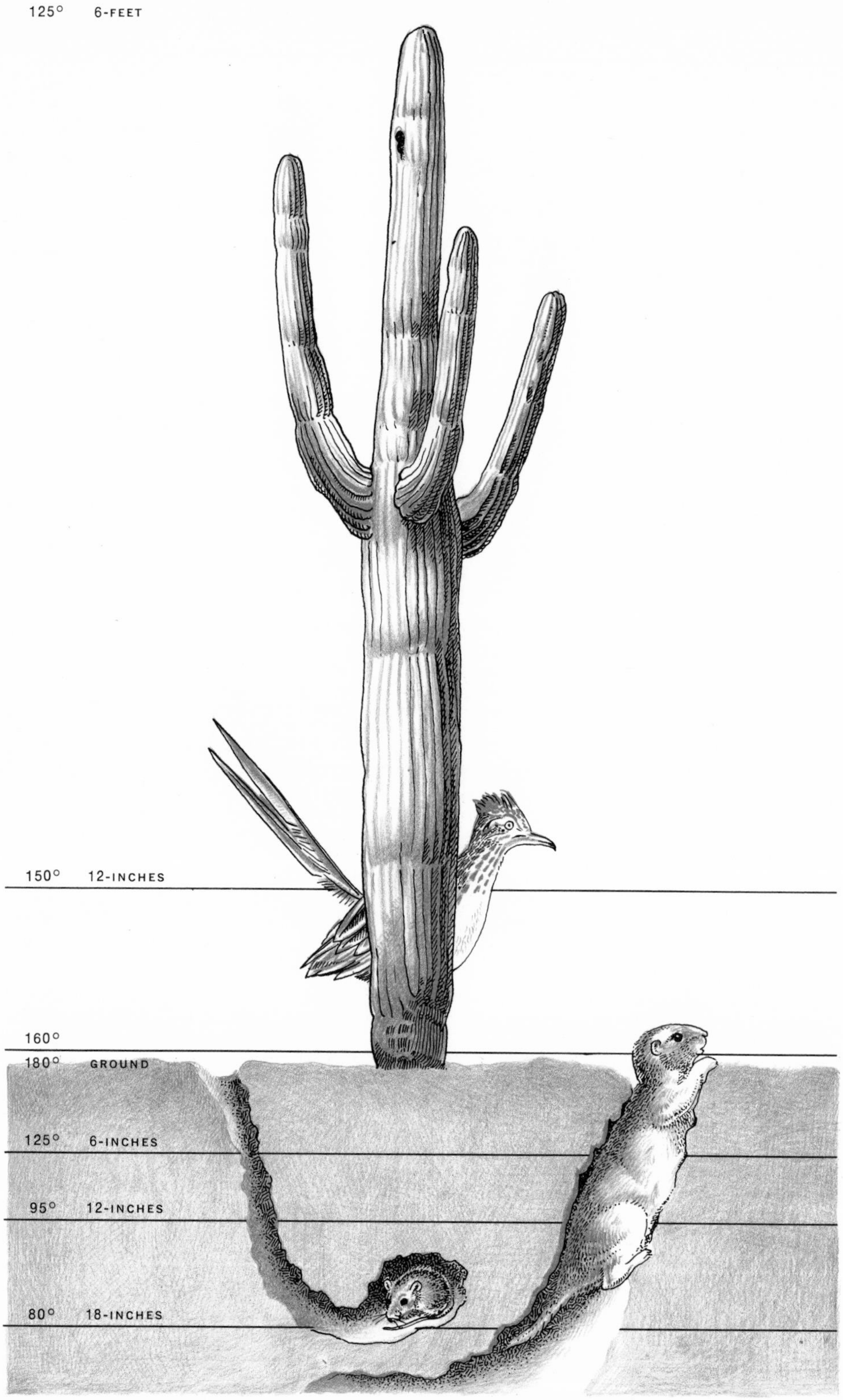

125°   6-FEET

150°   12-INCHES

160°
180°   GROUND

125°   6-INCHES

95°   12-INCHES

80°   18-INCHES

Of course these ratios of heat penetration, or lack of it, vary with ground cover, for the sun's rays have potential heat only when encountering an object. If the object encountered is white or light colored, most of the rays bounce off with almost no transformation. If dark, the rays are absorbed and the heat is added to for as long as the light is present. As a result, the heat generated by the sun's rays on dark ground penetrates a little deeper than it does on light terrain. A simple test can prove the point. This time take two pans of shallow water. In one immerse a circle of white paper, and in the other a circle of black, and then set both in the sun. A short time later the black-papered water will almost cook an egg.

This desert tendency toward lighter colored living things than those usually found in forested areas, can therefore serve a double purpose. It not only gives the animals protective coloration but also hinders their absorption of heat. Whether the latter is an advantage to the pure white pornuba moth is questionable, however, because of the insect's nocturnal habits. This insect's white color, when perched on pure white yucca blooms, is one of the greatest matches in all nature, just as its astounding system of blossom fertilization is unique in the animal world, a perfect example of symbiosis. Without the moth the yucca could not exist, and without the yucca neither could the moth.

There are many methods by which plants are fertilized. On coniferous trees it is done almost entirely by wind, with chance gusts picking up pollen and in a hit-or-miss method dropping some where they will fertilize the plants. The blooms of most other plants, however, offer something of value to insects in the way of food, such as nectar or pollen. These blooms are placed in such a position that stamens and pistils both must be touched as an insect enters or leaves the flower. A few plants just pretend to offer food by emitting an alluring odor of something desirable but which really does not exist. So, in almost every case where insects are required for cross-fertilization, they either receive a reward or are promised one which during pollination they cannot find.

The tiny white moth that fertilizes the yucca does not receive any of these inducements. Instead it goes to work with a complicated series of maneuvers which almost points toward intelligence and thought rather than the blind instinct that motivates it. Yuccas are similar to the century plant mentioned in the second chapter, in that they have a rapidly growing flowering stalk which erupts from the center of the plant in the spring of the year. Upon reaching the prescribed height, a candle-like series of blooms opens at the top. They will withstand the weather for a few weeks, then wither. By autumn the same stalk will support a number of woody pods which split open and scatter their seeds on the ground. This same series of events occurs, with variations, on many plants. From flower to seed to dispersal is customary in the botanical world. However, in almost every case where insects are employed to start this cycle of reproduction, it is the plant that makes the advances. The insect is just the means to carry the pollen.

During daylight hours the yucca moth rests amid the petals of the milk-white flower, and in the evening when the bloom reaches maturity it collects a ball of pollen from the anthers. Even though this ball is larger than the moth's head it is held under its chin as it makes its way to another blossom. There the female moth inserts several eggs about a third of the way down the pistil and, if she were the usual type of insect, her work would be done. But the pornuba then climbs to the stigma on the top of the same pistil and actually rubs the little ball of pollen, which was collected previously, into that part of the plant as though to ensure fertilization.

It is the collecting of this pollen and the act of rubbing it in that makes this insect unique, almost as though a thought process were at work. If the flowers were not fertilized—and it seems that only pornubas can do it—seeds would not develop in the seed pods and the eggs of the moth, after hatching, would starve to death. How the system originated has had scientists baffled. Suffice to say that it happens every spring and, as a result, there are pornubas flitting around yucca blossoms and

many yuccas on the desert with both plant and animal owing their existence to a unique type of symbiosis.

Another strange action of insects concerns the readying of a mesquite branch for its larva by the mesquite girdler. This however is parasitic, for although the insect benefits, the tree suffers. There are often perfectly healthy mesquite trees to be seen with a single branch dead or dying. If the season is right the tiny leaves will be withered, showing that life existed until a short time before. Dried-up leaves are commonly encountered on the broken branch of any tree, but on the mesquite branch there is no prominent sign of mutilation. Life just seems to be withheld from one special point on the bough, a point which if closely examined will reveal a tiny ring of bark and its underlying cambium layer removed. This is meticulously done, almost as though a craftsman with a chisel set at the desired depth had completely circled the branch circumference with a sixteenth of an inch groove. It is just deep enough to stop the flow of any life-sustaining sap to the outermost twigs. On a desert where every bit of moisture is at a premium the intentional killing of a branch is not customary.

However, the tiny long-horned beetle that does its precision girdling must carry on its race. After the death of the branch has been assured, the beetle drills tiny holes in the still-green bark, and inserts its eggs. The white grubs that hatch crisscross their wooden home with countless tunnels, and feed on the sugar which the deadwood supplies. Within a year they pupate and emerge through the bark, ready to start the cycle again.

This necessity for deadwood as food is not rare in the animal kingdom. However, as a general rule the animals that live upon it, such as the multitudes of termite species that are to be found on all deserts, center their attention on timber that is already dead. In this way they not only act as debris eliminators but also form the last important link in the food chain of life which we started with lichens.

The socialistic home life of termites is one of the marvels of nature and although they have been the subject of research for years, new facts are constantly being discovered. In some instances even their scientific nomenclature—the naming of the individual species—is based not on visible differences of external characters but on the infinitesimal protozoans within their bodies which are necessary for digestion of foods. This digestion results in tiny sawdust-like pellets being extruded. They either assimilate into and replenish the soil, or are used by the insects to build their complicated homes which even on the hottest deserts of the world have a remarkable control of humidity.

This delicate balance of life and death which eventually funnels every living thing back into the soil so that the chain may start again, takes still another form with the palo verde wood borer. This three-inch-long cousin of the tiny mesquite girdler also feeds on deadwood but its diet is a little more plebeian. The eggs are laid by the adult beetle at the base of the "green stick" tree, and upon hatching the tiny larva commences burrowing into the living roots. Before many weeks have passed the tunneling and feeding affect the health of the trunk above, and the tree eventually dies.

Two or three years after the grub's labors have killed a main trunk on the palo verde, the interior of the trunk is honeycombed by borings—tunnels which are the diameter of a dime and almost as round. Then the four-inch white body of the grub tunnels into the dirt where it was originally hatched and there develops into a large black beetle. Like so many insects its adult life is a very short one compared to its juvenile larval stage. Aside from mating to produce a future generation, its few weeks of life seem to be spent heading for and crashing into man-made lights, a reaction to human occupation which often cuts the beetle's short life even shorter.

And of all instinctive reactions, most of which have a definite place in survival, this one that causes a hopeless chasing of light is the hardest to understand, and on which to base a theory. The only reason known is the physiological one that causes some moths and other insects to be lured to their doom. Tests have shown that a strong light on one eye and dim on the other will cause the wing on the dim side to beat faster than the wing on the lighted side. As a result, the insect being lured is drawn to the target as inexorably as some of the military heat-sensing rockets are drawn to the distant warmth of an enemy airplane. But instincts developed through the ages rarely change, and never rapidly. Reason is not a part of their make-up and in a few cases irresistible impulses that might have saved lives in the past—now, in a different environment, have the opposite effect. If thought processes could change deep-rooted instincts, rattlesnakes would have stopped rattling when the first human beings invaded the Americas.

Chapter 6

Desert Snakes

Snakes are probably the most hated denizens of desert country, yet to most people they hold a peculiar fascination which is unequaled by any other animal group. Maybe it is the old Adam and Eve story, or even Cleopatra and the asp, that have stimulated this awe of reptiles, a feeling that makes the serpentarium of any zoo the most visited of all exhibits. This is not a fear that can in any way be called instinctive to the human race, for most psychologists claim that the fear of reptiles must be implanted at an early age and is then carried through life to a greater or lesser degree. Some people can become objective about reptiles through corrective education, but to many that fear, once implanted, cannot be changed. With such a mental curtain one of the most entrancing families in the over-all study of nature can be lost to otherwise curious minds.

Rattlesnakes are found all the way from southern Canada through the tropics and on to South America. Some species, and there are about fifty in North America alone, are residents of mountain ranges. Others have not only adapted to swampy areas but also to the driest and hottest of our deserts. Being cold-blooded and devoid of sweat glands, they are at the mercy of weather extremes and as their temperature tolerances are from slightly above freezing to about one hundred degrees Fahrenheit, their adjustments to the varied habitats have been many. Those in the north and on the cold high mountain ranges probably spend about half of their lives in deep underground hibernation, while their relatives in mild temperature belts to the south are abroad both day and night throughout the year. Most of the desert varieties go through a four- or five-month hibernation but upon emerging have even further restrictions—being forced by lethal daylight temperatures to confine their foraging to the night.

Being able to hunt in total darkness is an ability possessed by several animals. Some owls have developed such sensitive ears that they can successfully hear a rodent's scamperings on dry leaves and thus catch mice without using their eyes. Bats in total darkness emit a sound from the mouth which, upon hitting an object, bounces back to the supersensitive ears carrying a message of distance, direction, and size. The pit vipers, however, to which family the rattlesnakes belong, utilize a different principle based on the emission of the heat that is constantly given off by all warm-blooded animals.

The snake has two pits, situated between the nostrils and eyes. They are temperature nerve centers guiding the reptile's strike to its destination. Without these highly developed nerves for the detection of warmth, rattlesnakes would be in a bad way, for their eyesight is not only poor, but their hearing, as we know it, is non-existent. But as if to counteract this last deficiency, their bodies seem supersensitive to ground vibrations, a sensitivity that alerts them to the approach of enemy or prey even though its position is such that it cannot be seen or sensed by its warmth.

Their greatest development, however, centers on their poison-injecting apparatus, which is also possessed by other reptilian families all over the world. At the base of the jaws there are two poison glands which tend to give the heads of rattlers a triangular appearance. (This shape, however, is not a general recognition mark for all poisonous snakes.) These sacks or glands have a duct running forward, and just under the nostrils it connects to needle-sharp hollow fangs which, on a large rattler, can be up to three-quarters of an inch in length. When the mouth is closed the fangs are hinged to lie snugly along the roof, but when it is opened for striking they arch forward with pointed ends positioned to precede the lunge. At the moment that they penetrate the flesh of food or enemy, a contraction of the glands forces poison through the ducts and out the tiny slots near the tip ends of these hypodermic-like teeth.

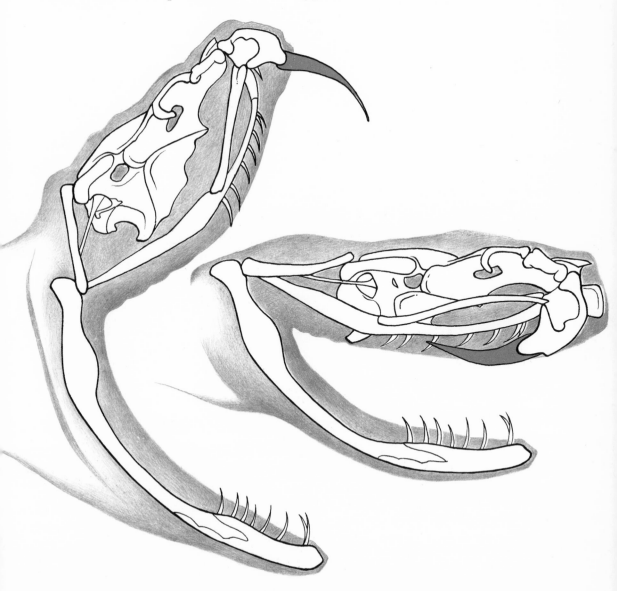

The composition of the snake's poison varies with each species of rattlesnake. Injections from some result in rapid coagulation of the blood of the animal bitten and death is caused by a clotting and stoppage of the circulation of veins and arteries. Other species have venom that works in reverse by causing massive hemorrhages that break down tissues. Some have venoms which are largely neurotoxic, damaging nerves and paralyzing the victim's respiratory system. But in spite of all these unpleasant results of a bite, comparatively few people die after being bitten. Although statistics vary, it is generally conceded that bites from the average rattlesnake on an average sized human being result in only about one death in ten, even without medical treatment. With medical treatment the percentage drops the fatalities to 1 or 2 per cent.

The primary reason for the venom is not the killing of enemies but the procurement of food. In spite of their lethal bite, rattlesnakes, like most other animals, do not seek battle just for the sake of conflict. If they can profit by biting, such as in procuring food or in eliminating an enemy that is blocking escape, they will use their fangs. The high incidence of bites inflicted on snake handlers versus the low incidence of bites incurred in the wild, tends to prove their non-belligerent nature. In captivity the snakes cannot get away, but when free they use their venom only as a last resort—when escape is impossible.

As an example of getting food with almost no danger to the predator, the venomous snakes hold an enviable position in the animal world. A single quick strike at a passing morsel, followed by an instant recoil, has far less danger than the grasp and wrestle technique used by non-venomous reptiles. After the instantaneous injection, small prey such as mice or rats will often succumb within a few inches of where they were, but rabbits will sometimes run off out of the sight range of the snake before being affected.

Very little of this disappearing food is lost, for the tongues of snakes are their organs of smell and, judging from the way they are used, they are most efficient. On one occasion members of the staff at Tucson's Arizona-Sonora Desert Museum found a dead rabbit at least twenty feet from any logical hiding place for a rattlesnake. Fang marks showed the cause of death. After the rabbit's removal, a diamondback was seen scouring the area with head moving from side-to-side and with black-tipped tongue constantly testing the ground at the exact spot where the rabbit had died. If the natural sequence of events had not been broken by human interference, the act of a small snake swallowing a creature several times its girth would have demonstrated another almost unbelievable adaptation of reptiles.

Our jaws and the jaws of other mammals, birds, lizards, and fishes, have a single hinge spot on each side of the head. This permits all these creatures to swing their jaws in a downward arc which mightily enlarges the mouth opening but does not alter the opening from mouth to throat. Therefore, morsels either have to be small, or the animal must be capable of chewing in order to chop up the food into swallowable pieces. Snakes, due to needle-sharp teeth which puncture but cannot cut, are incapable of chewing and were it not for their possession of extra bones connecting the jaw to the rest of the skull, food intake would be difficult if not impossible.

These bones, known as the squamosal and quadrate, lie horizontally when the mouth of the snake is shut and can maintain that position if the mouth is opened. In the act of swallowing a large morsel, however, they assume a vertical position which not only enlarges the throat opening four or five times greater than normal but makes swallowing possible.

All snakes have rows of teeth on the roof and floor of the mouth which are completely independent of the poison-injecting mechanism. The sharp tips of these point toward the throat, making it for all purposes a one-way street with easy entrance but painful exit. The strange combination of squamosal and quadrate bones makes possible a pendulum action by the lower jaw, forcing the teeth ahead and pulling them back to a point beyond their normal "shut mouth" position. As the jaw is forced forward, the prey that is loosely gripped by the points of the

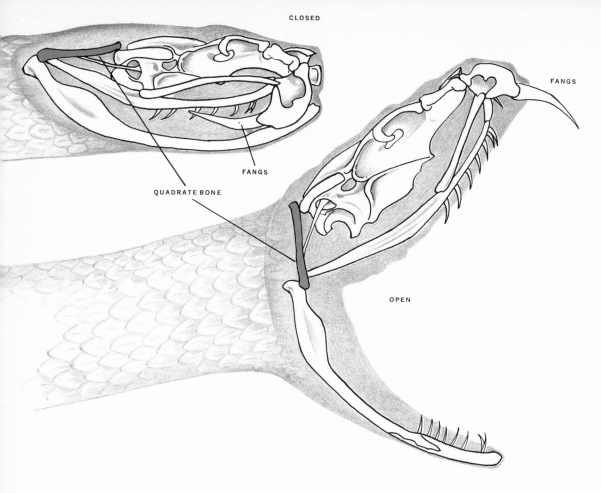

FANGS

FANGS

QUADRATE BONE

OPEN

upper teeth slides on the lower. But when the jaw is pulled backward—it is the lower recurved teeth that grip while the prey slides on the upper. Then there is a terrific expansion of the skin and the throat area and on down the body as a super-large prey is ingested.

As the snake grows there comes a time when the outer skin can stretch no further and separates from a brand new and larger skin beneath. When this casting off of the old and wearing of the new is about to occur, the eyes become opaque and the snake rubs its lips against rough surfaces until the nose plates break loose. From then on the loose skin is caught on any protuberance and turns inside-out as it peels off clear to the tail. With each shedding made by rattlesnakes, a new rattle segment is added to the existent string. However, as there can be from one to six sheddings in a single year, it is impossible to tell the age of a rattler by counting its rattles.

It is thought that once rattles were used to warn animals of danger, thus making them avoid the immediate territory occupied by the reptile. In the days when buffalo and antelope roamed parts of the West in unbelievable numbers, the ability to give an audible warning probably prevented many snakes from being trampled upon. But conditions that had remained almost static for ages, changed drastically in the last few hundred years as civilized man, a killer for sport, altered not only the habitat but also the animal ecology. Now, instead of a rattle that warns away another animal, its attention-attracting noise can bring it instant death.

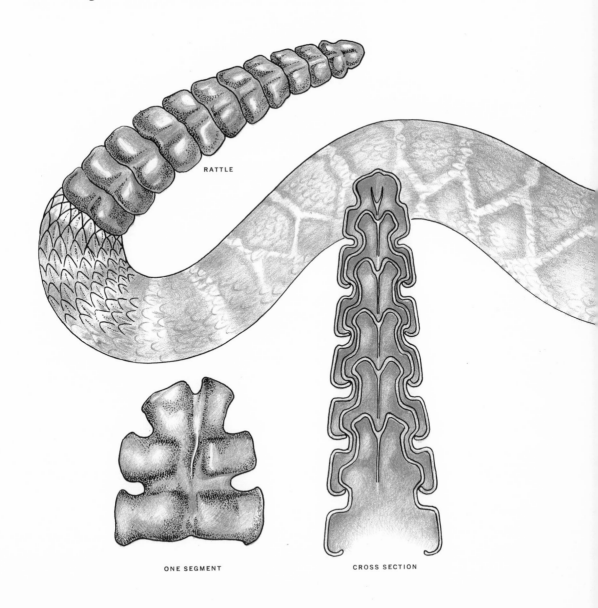

RATTLE

ONE SEGMENT

CROSS SECTION

This change in reaction has been sudden—far too fast for the snake to adapt to the disappearance of hoofed animals and the advent of human beings in the territory inhabited by rattle-snakes. However, there are two tiny islands in the Gulf of California where hoofed animals have never existed and rattle-snakes have been isolated for many thousands of generations. Plenty of time and the sea birds that live on these islands are now forcing a reversal in the evolution of the rattle, for here it is not only a useless appendage but a distinct disadvantage to survival. Those snakes that through individual disposition or possibly faulty rattles did not make a noise, were more apt to be overlooked by hungry birds—so in a very broad sense the quiet ones lived to breed and the noisy ones didn't. In time a freakish gene appeared which eliminated the grooves which held the additional segments after each shedding. Now, on the lonely islands of Catalina and San Lorenzo, that instinct to shake a tail when disturbed is still retained by the snakes but genetics have done away with the rattle.

Throughout the world of nature color has a great bearing on survival, going far beyond the obvious such as the white bears on the icecap, and black ones in the dark forests. Color when combined with pattern can create unbelievable illusions. Strangely, some of the designs that protect are patterns that draw attention. The snakeskins of the western deserts have three basic designs. There are the ringed ones with contrasting bands encircling the body. There are the striped ones with ribbons of color running from head to tail. Then there are the mottled ones which, of the three, blend best into a variety of backgrounds. Such drastic differences of pattern provide a form of protective coloration about which little is known by the general public, for it relies not on camouflage but on deception, a deception that would be unworkable if all three color variations did not exist.

Compared to birds and mammals, snakes are not fast. The rattlers are so sluggish that their top speed would probably not exceed three miles an hour. Even the racers, speed demons of the family, have not been clocked above eight. But despite these speeds, easily exceeded by all their enemies, snakes are difficult to catch—based on the fact that their patterns so falsify their movements that split-second judgments of speed are confusing. All forward motion of any of the ringed snakes puts a light band where a dark one had been just seconds before. This not only deliberately attracts notice but gives an optical illusion of speed considerably faster than reality. Hence the "lead" of a pouncing hawk or fox hits the presumed point of contact before the ringed snake has arrived.

If all snakes were ringed the experiences of a few misses could correct this miscalculation. But assume that the next snake seen by the predator is one with lengthwise stripes which, when in progress, give no sharp change from one contrasting color to another. Instead there is a flow of motion somewhat similar to that seen on a barber's pole, or better yet—that seen on a spinning top. In reality the same speed is there but optically the motion is arrested. This time the dive of a hungry predator lands him behind his fleeing prey and he misses again. This is survival based on deceptive color and pattern, both of which work due to their variations. But either one might fail dismally if the other was not occasionally present to create a sense of indecision in split-second judgment.

Most snakes throughout the world travel across the ground with muscular undulations which run from head to tail on a horizontal plane. A sliding forward action is achieved by utilizing every branch or bulge on the ground which will prevent slippage in much the same manner that the keel of a sailboat achieves its tack. But some type of surface rigidity must be present to provide a forward motion. With the boat it is water fighting the sideways motion of the air, and with the ordinary run of snakes it is an uneven ground fighting the actions of the sinuous muscles which ripple from head to tail.

However, most deserts have dunes—those barren areas where the shifting sands are so light that they move with the vagaries of the winds, where even the small insects sink to their ankles. Here horizontal traction at best is poor, for each forward push dislodges sand backward. Only a vertically downward weight has stable footing and some of the reptiles of the dunes have almost mastered a partial air travel in a looping maneuver which leaves a peculiar series of disconnected parallel imprints across these seas of sand.

The chief examples of this mode of travel are the sidewinder rattlesnakes, a species rarely found far from loose sand where their tracks resemble miniature five-yard lines on a football field. Other snakes also inhabit these dune areas but most of them are burrowers, progressing under the soil rather than on the surface. When track comparisons can be made between the burrowers and the sidewinders, the efficiency of the latter's method is plainly evident. Each scale imprint stands out in sharp relief, showing that all slippage has been eliminated. By contrast, the burrowers that try surface travel heap up pressure ridges which are not only unfailing clues to their travel direction but, in a circumstantial way, show that energy is wasted when they try to move outside of their underground element.

Eventual perfection to fit habitat is a plan evident in all forms of life. As predators evolve better methods of catching prey, the prey—to survive—must develop improved evasive tactics. These changes are not short-termed projects but occupy many thousands and perhaps millions of years in the hit-or-miss method which tends to quarantine the unfit by death. In the last few hundred years, however, the thought processes of man have been able to cram the progression of ages into a relatively few centuries by a planned and complete elimination of what man considers unsuitable to his own needs and a preservation of those animals he wishes to foster. The expanding numbers of the breeds of dogs, cats, pigeons, and chickens prove this point. Some of these new animals are so outlandish that they could never survive without human help. However, their development shows what can be done in a historically brief time. In fact, nothing in nature is static, even when left to evolve by itself.

And, just as human beings, by utilizing their knowledge of

genetics, can almost fashion animals to suit their fancy, nature does the same in various parts of the world. So, back to sidewinders—this time as an example of parallel evolution. There are places in the western United States, in the Sahara, and in the great inland deserts of Australia, that are virtually interchangeable as far as topographical looks are concerned. In all three areas there are completely unrelated families of snakes. To survive, all three have developed pattern and locomotion characteristics so similar to our western sidewinders that they are almost indistinguishable.

Chapter 7
Adaptations

Although sidewinders and Sahara vipers are classics of parallel development, examples of theory occur in every group of animals and in many plant families. With weather a dominant factor in the shaping of terrain it is only natural that areas on widely separated continents develop along similar lines, either as forests, swamps, plains, or deserts, and on each there are living "look-alikes" that can survive only in their special environments. In short, every type of country has its own type of life and if duplicated environs occur on two or more continents there is a better than even chance that some of the living things of both will be externally similar.

This seems especially true in the case of some lizards of Australia and some in the western United States. In both countries terrain similarities are so astounding that great chunks of either land could be interchanged with almost no difference in over-all appearance. And if a human native of either continent were watching an anthill on the other continent when a flat, broad, heavily spined lizard approached for an insect meal, the

MOLOCH HORRIDUS

HORNED LIZARD

American would say, "Look! a horned toad," the Australian would say, "Look! a moloch."

If perchance the anthill was under a spiny plant, there could be another misidentification by the transplanted human beings. The Australian in America would call the cactus a euphorbia, while the American in Australia would call the euphorbia a cactus. Yet cactus in all its many varieties is native only to the Americas. So on these two continents we have totally unrelated plants and lizards that evidently progressed along similar lines since the start of time. Despite divergent origins they now look so much alike that from a short distance we can easily confuse one for the other.

And—on all four of these living things, the look-alike plants and look-alike lizards, spines are the armor which permits them to survive in their arid habitats by making them unpalatable to their many enemies. That such protection is effective is circumstantially proven by the sluggishness of both the lizards, for they are as slow or slower than any others in their respective families. So, if we assume that the sluggishness of turtles, rattlers, skunks, and porcupines is due to defenses which make speed unnecessary, then the defenses of horned toads and molochs must also be effective for the same reason.

However, what is adequate protection under prevailing circumstances can change and become detrimental when the ecology is altered. North America, home of the horned toads, had its ecology changed by human immigrants. Several hundred years later the horned toad population was also affected by man.

It happened this way. When it was found that the lizards known as horned toads were inoffensive, comparatively sluggish, and that they seemingly like to be handled, a call for the creatures as pets was broadcast. As this traffic seriously depleted their numbers, many thousands were shipped to wholesalers and then transshipped as singles or pairs to their final destinations—often to climates where they would become emaciated due to improper food and perish with the first cold winds of fall. Even though some species of horned toads have broods of a score or more, their reproduction and expendable surplus could not stand this drain. In parts of the West they virtually disappeared, especially around towns and cities where they were the most-sought-after of all reptiles.

This overharvesting of a region's animal life has happened many times in the past and, unfortunately, the danger of possible extermination is usually not realized until it is almost too late. It happened with desert tortoises in some of the arid parts of California, with antelope ground squirrels in some coastal valleys, and most certainly would have occurred with horned lizards if the farsighted Arizona Game and Fish Department had not enacted protective laws. Now the permits that are issued within the State of Arizona for the possession of these lizards are limited to accredited scientific or educational institutions.

Horned toads were protected because of the universality of their appeal. That is not the criterion, however, that gave protection to the Gila monster, the only poisonous reptile in the world to receive this distinction. The protection of a dangerous animal shows that the human race is gradually becoming aware of the right of any creature to live as long as it can and die a normal death. It also shows that the educational activities of conservationists are beginning to bear fruit. Perhaps in the future the wanton human destruction of animals that has exterminated several hundred different kinds in a few hundred years, will stop before an imbalance in nature occurs which can never be corrected.

The early settlers of the West concocted some strange, purely mythical stories about Gila monsters, all based indirectly on their supposed digestive systems. According to these tales the body refuse of the Gila monsters was expelled through the mouth and the resultant putrefaction caused not only the bite of the lizards to be deadly but also accredited their breaths with the power of causing headaches and nausea. In reality Gila monsters have digestive systems similar to all other vertebrate animals, and their poison apparatus feeds the venom from glands situated in their lower jaws.

Compared to the hypodermic-like fangs of rattlesnakes, the teeth of Gilas are primitive. Instead of being hollow for a pressure injection, they have small grooves which run to the poison glands and the venom seeps up much like ink from a fountain pen. With this system, unlike the customary strike and almost instant withdrawal of a rattler, the Gila grabs and chews with a grip that is hard to break.

Drop for drop, Gila monster poison is thought to be as lethal as that injected by some species of rattlers. However, the retiring inoffensive nature of these lizards, combined with the necessity for chewing, makes them one of the least dangerous of all venomous reptiles. Most if not all of the bites received by man have been inflicted on people handling Gilas. If left alone these lizards are not dangerous. They never initiate an attack and their presence on the western deserts adds another bit of bright color to the desert land. They would be sorely missed if unreasonable fear caused them to be eliminated.

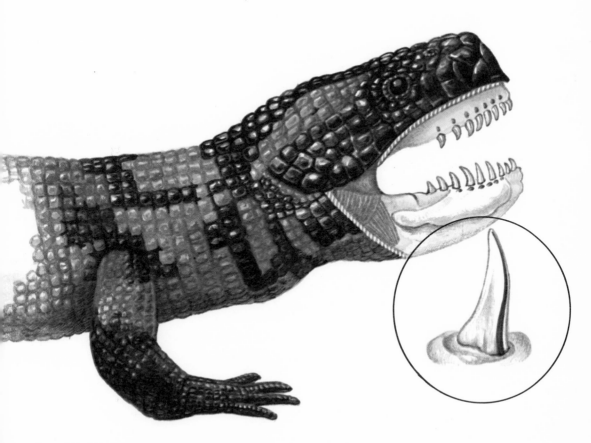

The chuckwalla, the second largest lizard on our western deserts, has developed other methods of escaping hungry predators. Their survival is based on a combination of color pattern, choice of home, and inflatable bodies. In color they break the desert rule of a tendency toward lightness, for their preferred habitat is in the jumbled black boulders spewed out by long-extinct volcanoes. To match such a home they are generally two-toned, with the head end of the body almost as black as the rocks upon which they climb. The tail end is usually lighter, almost verging on yellow—to match the drifting yellow sands which seep between the boulders, forming beds for the vegetation upon which the lizards feed.

Two-toned coloration is an effective camouflage for some animals under some circumstances, for it tends to break the quick recognition of what otherwise would be a familiar form. A chuckwalla sitting on a black lava boulder does not show up in its entirety, for the only part that draws attention is the light-colored tail. To a highflying hawk or a hungry coyote this streak of light might seem to be a rock stain, a drifted bit of sand, or a wind-blown bit of bleached bark. The same chuckwalla on the sand dune between the rocks would appear as a tailless black object, hardly worth a second glance. On either the black rock

or yellow sand background, the outline of a familiar serpent figure would be lost. Possibly the deception would last for only a second, but for animal survival, tiny fractions of time can mean the difference between life and death.

Suppose for a moment, however, that the predator in search of a lizard meal detects the deception (some do successfully, or we would be knee-deep in chuckwallas), and makes a rapid dash at the now fleeing lizard. Piles of lava boulders on all sides offer sanctuary. But the "chuck" has one niche in particular which is reached just in the nick of time. Although there are many deep hiding places, a narrow crack—an inch and a half high by a little more than a foot in length—is his final destination. Almost before his motion stops he inflates his body by taking deep breaths until the rough scaly back and his smoother belly become wedged into the crevice so tightly that he could be removed only by lifting the rock. The hawk or coyote becomes frustrated —dinner in sight, almost reachable, but impossible to remove with the tools that either predator has available.

Most of these lava rocks that harbor a tremendous population of chuckwallas, erupted long ago from the scores of craters that dot the Pinacate region near Organ Pipe Cactus National Monument. The area is unbearably hot in the summer months and

most plants and animals utilize their own special adaptations to beat this heat. If visited in spring or fall it is a living textbook on protective coloration for the ground is a crazy quilt of color running the gamut from black to white.

When almost stepped upon—a granite colored lizard known as the desert iguana puts on a burst of speed and disappears. Although glimpsed fleetingly he is a "normal" with color similar to others of his kind wherever deserts are normal also. Disturbed horned toads are typical too. As long as their mottled flat bodies with brownish pattern remain motionless, they remain unseen.

The lava fields are sharply outlined because of their blackness—a color character of the soil due to ages of wind erosion on the lava boulders where the chuckwallas reside. These acres, too, are the home of smaller lizards. In size, shape, and even in actions these lizards are similar to those mentioned before. Now, however, they look as though they had been faintly sprayed with black so they are as hard to see as the others encountered back on the normal trail.

There is a half mile of this speckled black lava soil. Then there appears another sharp line of demarcation caused by drifting white sands covering the black. As this boundary is approached a faint change in the lizards is detectable, for the speckled black spray effect becomes grayer. When the dunes are reached and for a hundred yards on all sides, the so-called normals are most numerous. As dunes take over from the black soil, however, the lizards tend toward whiteness, a color giving them protection in this new environment.

In this color laboratory, caused by a seething volcanic inferno of ages past, some interesting experiments could be made. Mentally separate the soils into three sections such as the blackest of the dark, the whitest of the dunes, and the transitional that separates these two extremes. Place a lizard from the latter, a so-called "normal," on the black and although he will be hard to see he obviously shows up more prominently than those that are permanent residents. Vice versa, place him on the white and the same effect will be noticed. Next, take one from the black and place him on the white, and one from the white and place him on the black. These would stand out like sore thumbs and as a result would become instant prey to the first predator that entered the area.

Although this color laboratory of the Pinacates demonstrates the survival benefits of camouflage, there is still a question as to whether or not the individual reptiles are aware that they are on matching or unmatching soil. But this much is sure—one on an unmatched situation boldly advertises his whereabouts, and would probably be killed before he could reproduce.

The ability to conceal is characteristic of almost all wild life. Very few living creatures flaunt their presence before another species unless they are sure of a friendly reception or are powerful enough to overcome opposition should it occur. Most desert valleys of the West, however, are inhabited by a tiny lizard that seemingly never heard of these common-sense rules. At the first sign of disturbance their toothpick legs will lift their bodies from the ground and the long tapering tail will rise over the back and start wagging back and forth. Such actions show the

GRID-TAILED LIZARD

startling black and white bands on its underside from which the reptile derives the name zebra or grid-tailed lizard. It is a strange show of bravado and were it not for the fact that they are extremely fast and also have adequate protective coloration on their upper surfaces, the trait could be detrimental.

However, a logical explanation for the tail semaphoring of the zebra tail lizard has yet to be explained. Look at the facts as they appear to a casual observer and try to emerge with a "why." The zebra tail is a small lizard of from five to maybe six inches in length. The entire surface of its back from the tip of its nose to the end of its tail, is faintly blotched with a subdued pattern on a sandy colored background that perfectly matches the soil upon which it normally lives. Its running speed is fantastic when all four legs are used, and when it really wishes to turn on speed its body forms a half-circle arc, achieving propulsion with the hind legs alone. The zebra tail gives the effect of flying without leaving the ground. Either attribute, coloration or speed, could give it adequate protection from its enemies.

It is in its use of these attributes, however, that the zebra tail seemingly contradicts common-sense survival. The protective coloration of the back runs to ground level and when this surface is reached, switches to a creamy white on the underside of the chin and belly. From the hind legs backward to the tip of the tail this white of the under surface is boldly marked with black bands, so prominent that if a zebra tail lizard was placed on his back in his normal habitat he could be seen for a hundred feet or more.

But it does have speed, a quick reaction to the approach of an enemy, and one more unusual ability. When the lizard is caught, sometimes it escapes—but in escaping is forced to play its ace card—a detachable tail.

Tails that detach from the body of a lizard occur on many of the desert species. Some take a strong tug to achieve breakage. Others, such as those on geckos, a small elliptical-pupiled night lizard, can seemingly disconnect at the animal's will. As a survival technique they evidently serve a good purpose for about

fifty per cent of all geckos caught by man show that there has been a regrowth of a lost tail.

Break-away jerseys are often used in football. A tackler grabbing one would end up with a handful of cloth and a runner being tackled would continue bare shouldered for a touchdown. The breakable tails of lizards work the same way, for they are often the first appendage to be grasped by a predator. When the tail breaks loose it wiggles and squirms for seconds, making the predator feel that he is about to have a complete dinner. The main body of the lizard, however, keeps right on going. Within a month or so a new tail regenerates, ready to be sacrificed to save a life a second time.

The regrowth of expendable tails, running on hind legs only, the black on black and white on white, and bodies that inflate, all prolong life for the desert lizards—each in its individual way. But for real diversification all crowded into one animal, a fringe-foot lizard may be the champion. It lives in barren areas consisting of the driest and finest of sand, so powdery that it shifts with the faintest breeze and each step on an uphill grade ends with a backward slide.

Man has tried to conquer the dunes in many ways, even to the point of introducing flatfoot camels as beasts of burden. When that failed, a strange corduroy road was constructed. It consisted of four by six planks wired together with one-inch spaces between each timber. In theory this serpentine undulating highway, the bumpiest one in the world, floated on the sands. When covered by drifts it could be lifted to the surface again by being pried to the top. Remnants of it still are to be seen on the dunes west of Yuma, Arizona.

Man has recently traveled across these barren sandy wastes in another way, this time by cutting the center out of old cars until they are almost square, and equipping them with oversized airplane tires which are two or three times normal width. On Sundays these strange vehicles careen over the rolling sands, driven by students with goggles, ear muffs, and in some cases face masks to protect themselves from the swirling gritty dust.

In many ways the fringefoot lizards, which today spend some of their time ducking the dune buggies, could have been the patterns for these gasoline monsters. As the name "fringefoot" implies, their feet have fringelike scales radiating from each toe. Like oversized tires, these prevent sinking and permit the lizards to dash speedily away at the approach of an enemy. Even in such an escape their actions are tuned to the environment, for their route invariably heads them for the steepest side of one of the piles of loose and powdery sand. With no perceptible slowdown they hit it at its base and the covering avalanche gives protection for as long as they wish to stay.

However, this type of hiding which works so well for fringefoots could be a graveyard for most other animals, because the sand, although slightly coarser than powdered sugar, seeps insidiously into the slightest opening. By all the rules of the game, lungs, ears, and eyes should be so packed with it that hearing and sight would be sadly impaired. But like the buggy drivers with goggles and masks the fringefoots have equipment also. The nostrils have special valves that can close tightly while the ears have flaps that sand pressure will force to a shut position. The mouth has overhanging upper lips that work in the same way, and the eyes have serrated lids like the teeth of two saws which lock and form an impenetrable seal. In combination all these specialties work so well in fact that the home environment preferred by fringefoots is shunned by most other creatures.

Chapter 8

Birds of the Desert

Just why a hot dry desert environment should have caused two birds, the cactus wren and the road runner, to be the most numerous members of their respective families is anyone's guess. These birds have so radically changed their family traits that they are almost unrecognizable if compared to their nearest of kin. Most cuckoos (the family to which the road runners belong) and most wrens are migratory, often flying great distances to winter in southern areas far from the territories where they were raised. But a road runner is not an average cuckoo, which normally is a streamlined bird with a body about the size of a robin that spends little if any time on the ground.

This desert representative of the family is almost pheasant size, completely sedentary, and rarely gets more than a few feet off the ground. As for the cactus wren, he, too, has a body almost robin size. But all the rest of the wren family are midgets, easily recognized by the carrying of their short tails over their backs, and usually nesting in trees or rock cavities.

The cactus wren, nonconformist that it is, builds nests that are bulky domed-over accumulations of grasses, twigs, and feathers, and as though to deny the fact that it is a wren, carries its tail straight out just like an ordinary bird. But a few traits typical of its smaller relatives are still retained, for like the marsh wrens and a few other members of the family, cactus wrens are not satisfied with just a single nest. They build throughout the year. As soon as one nest is completed they begin work on another. As a result of this boundless energy, a group of cholla plants selected as wren territory gives the appearance of housing a colony of the birds instead of just a single pair. And, as with most colonizing birds, such as casiques and weavers, there does not seem to be any real effort to hide their many homes by a careful selection of blending materials. Instead they take whatever is available. In cotton growing regions their white nests placed among the spines of green cholla are visible for hundreds of feet.

The preference that cactus wrens have for selecting thorny plants for nesting sites, combined with their multiple dwellings, may well have dulled a natural precautionary shyness. Although so many nests are visible, only one contains eggs or young birds. Predators become discouraged after a few non-productive painful searches. The use of decoys by various forms of wild life is not unknown. Some of the moths, fishes, and reptiles of the world have markings which make the tail end look like a head —fooling an enemy into attacking a non-vital area.

Many naturalists feel that the brighter colors of most male birds have decoy possibilities which, although detrimental to the particular individual parent, are a benefit to the species. By flaunting bright colors he could draw an enemy away from a nest and even though his life would be lost in the ruse, the somber-colored female could carry on the household duties. Circumstantial evidence in studies made on phalaropes gives some credence to this theory. These birds, which migrate through the desert on their way to prairie nesting grounds, have the customary sexual color pattern reversed; the male is the somber one while the female is brightly colored. She, of course, lays the

eggs, but incubation and the raising of the young then become the duty of the male while she, with her attractive colors, takes on the role of a protective decoy.

There is even a type of a decoy used by the road runner. Although this bird is omnivorous, living on scorpions, centipedes, insects, rodents, lizards, fruits, and small birds throughout most of the year, there are seasons when young rattlesnakes are on the menu. As a bite from even the young is lethal, there is a distinct danger whenever such food is caught and killed. During the ages which passed in making the changes from normal cuckoo to road runner physique, the body grew larger, wings became smaller, until the bird of the present is almost grounded. And although the typical cuckoo toe arrangement of two forward and two backward remained the same, the legs lengthened, becoming the primary means of travel and consequently more muscular than when it was a flying bird.

Although the wings have degenerated, making the bird practically a terrestrial creature, a new use for them has developed. Now they work in conjunction with the tail as windbreaks to aid in making the sharp turns and quick stops so necessary when in pursuit of agile lizards and rodents. In the capture of rattlers they seem to be used as capes are used by bullfighters. However, where the matador relies on playing the bull until it tires, the road runner is aided by the bright desert sun which can kill a reptile in a very few minutes. Except for those relatively few days in the early spring or fall when temperatures hover around seventy-five degrees, most desert snakes retreat underground soon after the sun rises above the horizon and do not emerge again until dusk. It is in the early morning hours when there is a slight overlap in the hiding of rattlers and the start of a new day for birds, that rattler versus bird bouts are usually seen.

The time is early morning with the sun casting long shadows

on the ground, causing temperatures to rise perceptibly with the passing of each minute. A fifteen-inch rattler, a product of the previous year, pushes its way across the ground, but just before reaching the shade of a bush, it is abruptly grabbed by the tail and thrown to the center of an open space. His three or four tail segments commence a furious buzzing while the body coils and the neck assumes an S-shaped position.

With the reptile in this pose, the bird that pulled him from a shady sanctuary shows more caution. Its tail of long feathers spreads and contracts like a fan and the short rounded wings open and shut spasmodically as the bird circles the reptile. Each revolution brings the two creatures closer together and then there is the first strike. Quick as it is, the wing is faster and the fangs sink harmlessly into the spread feathers which protect the bird's body from danger.

Strike follows strike and then, as the futility of the battle becomes apparent, the reptile again straightens out and heads for a nearby bush. With the snake's defensive pose abandoned, the road runner grabs the tail again and once more flips the reptile toward the clearing. More strikes follow, but they soon lose their original accuracy and become lunges of desperation. Each pulling back of the head becomes slower, and when slowed down enough it becomes the target for pecks from the sharp-pointed bill. How much of this increasing lethargy is due to tiring and how much is due to the build-up of heat from the rising sun cannot be figured. But there soon comes a time when the recoil from its strike is missing and the reptile lies helplessly on the ground.

With a lightning-like movement the snake's head is grasped in the bill and a powerful neck motion of the bird thrashes its body upon the ground. While a reflex action of the dying muscles is still twitching the reptile's tail, the bird begins to swallow the snake. The head, the neck, and about two-thirds of the snake's body disappear rapidly, but then comes a time when there is no more room. For another thirty or forty minutes the tail end dangles out of the bird's mouth while digestive juices disintegrate

118

the part of the meal already eaten and make room for the rest.

In addition to rattlers, the road runners eat eggs and the young of other birds. A road runner can dash into a family of baby quail and devour two or three before the rest of the brood escapes. That such a bird should be a benefactor of any species of quail seems incongruous to most people, but take a look at the facts.

For two or three months of the year baby quail and quail eggs are available if the road runner can find the eggs or fight off guarding parents and catch some of their chicks. Throughout the rest of the year quail are completely off the menu. For a full twelve months, however, mice, pack rats, and other rodents are a regular item of the road runner's diet and for about half a year red or black racer snakes are preyed upon. Pack rats, mice, and other rodents also take eggs whenever found. And the main food of the racer snakes during the nesting season consists of the eggs of wild birds. So if the time element is considered, road runners do far more good than harm for even though they are enemies of individual quail, they benefit the species by killing the predators of quail.

In nature nothing is all good or all bad. If we carefully study any living thing, a reason for its existence will eventually be found—possibly not from the human standpoint, but for the over-all continued existence of a balanced world. This is especially true in regard to the various woodpeckers which live in desert areas, even though many human residents fervently wish they would become extinct. This reaction is understandable. Their incessant drumming on water coolers at five o'clock in the morning, their drilling of holes in the giant saguaro cactus that has just been moved in at tremendous expense to enhance the appearance of a patio, their perforation of the wood trim of a house—which continues even after the scars have been covered with tin, does not make them popular birds around desert communities, despite the fact that they are most important keys to the bird ecology of the region.

If these woodpeckers were ever eliminated we could probably

struggle along for many years without feeling their absence, for their work of drilling holes in saguaros would be visible for as long as these cacti live. In time, however, new plants would take the place of the old ones. As those that showed signs of past woodpecker work crashed to the ground, the colonies of other birds that had used the holes for nesting sites would be forced to leave. With no birds to eat insects, the insects would reproduce at a fantastic rate. The absence of a single link in this chain—the woodpecker—would show disastrous results. Although the above is hypothetical and will probably never happen in the vast desert regions, if it did, it is conceivable that insects would take over.

A true situation similar to this hypothetical forecast occurred on one of the small islands of the Pacific. There, however, barn owls instead of woodpeckers were the supposed culprits because when they foraged over the island at night they occasionally snatched baby chicks. This island, a British possession known as Lord Howe Island, is a narrow one, hardly a dot on a map. Its main industry was the raising and export of a small species of ornamental palm which was adaptable to life in hotel lobbies and reception halls. As the owls had no place to hide, the campaign of extermination was remarkably successful and for several years there were almost no barn owls on the island. Their midnight screechings did not keep people awake and the few chicken farmers elatedly thought that their troubles were over.

Then the unbalance created by the extermination started to show in an abnormal increase of rats. Seedling palm trees were girdled or gnawed until exports of this product dropped dangerously low. Rats—the normal food of the owls—started working in increased numbers and with increased frequency on chicken eggs and pullets. With the economy ruined, the island appealed for help to England, and that government appealed to the United States which, in turn, requested help from the San Diego Zoo. Dozens of young barn owls were shipped to replace those so foolishly killed off and from last reports their offspring have reduced the rats to normal numbers and the island has recovered its original balance.

We must think before we eliminate a necessary link in nature's chain, for in ecology it works best unbroken. Here on the desert a dearth of woodpeckers would cause a scarcity or perhaps a complete disappearance of the following species of birds: sparrow hawks, screech owls, and elf owls. All three of these birds feed to a great extent on insects; the first two also eat small rodents, while the elf, the world's smallest owl, makes scorpions about 50 per cent of its diet. About three kinds of flycatchers nest in holes in saguaros. They live on low-flying insects and have been known to feed such food to their young every fifteen minutes throughout a day. Purple martins patrol the skies high above the ground and live on the tiny gnats and other pests which vary their altitude of activity depending on the heat, the humidity, and the time of day.

The influx of human beings to desert areas has vitally changed its bird population, decreasing some to a present status of rarity, and increasing others to almost pest proportion. Where men settle, habitats change, and some species of wild life are not able to adjust to the new condition.

One of Arizona's greatest losses was in the extermination of the masked bobwhite, a black-headed red-breasted species of quail that inhabited grasslands in a few valleys in southern Arizona. It was the sacred bird of the Papago Indians and was never used by that tribe as food. But throughout the early years of the American expansion an estimated twelve million cattle were driven from Mexico to American markets. In their journey they were forced to feed on the grasses where the birds lived. These herds not only ate the surface grass but so badly trampled the roots that the summer rains eroded them out of the ground and the verdant valleys became desert wastes. This caused the passing of the masked bobwhite from the Arizona scene.

Other birds fared better, however. This is especially true of two of the four species of doves which occur on the desert. The

Inca, one of the smallest of the family, was evidently a very rare bird in pioneer days, residing almost exclusively around Indian villages where water was available. With the advent of the towns and cities that now dot the countryside, with their increased water supply, the population of this dove has increased a thousand-fold.

Mourning doves have adapted to the changed habitats even more wholeheartedly, wintering in the agricultural areas in unbelievable thousands. Despite the fact that a ten-a-day hunter's limit and a two months' open season is a drain on their population, they do not seem to decrease in numbers. It is felt by many people that if given complete protection their attacks on the grain fields would soon place them in the depredation category which would permit their year-round eradication by holders of permits. Although mourning doves lay only two eggs to a clutch, one wild pair—nesting on the grounds of Tucson's Desert Museum—has raised seven broods of twins in a single season. This is a far greater production success than that achieved by most quail that lay a dozen or more eggs at a nesting.

Even though mourning doves usually live in desert areas they are wide-ranging birds, found from the Atlantic to the Pacific, north to Canada, and far into southern Mexico. However, the whitewings, a larger cousin, have not only definite desert limitations but their visits are controlled by the budding, flowering, and fruiting of the saguaros. If one of these phases in the reproduction cycle does not occur, the whitewings forsake the United States deserts for comparable areas in Mexico where plant reproduction cycles continue throughout the winter. This plant dependency brings them into Arizona in early April and they leave for their southern journey about the first of September, the day when Arizona's dove hunting season opens.

During their half-year stay they spend much of their time on the tops of the giant saguaro cacti, examining and occasionally opening the buds. When the flowers appear with their white petals and yellow centers, the doves then work on them, forcing their heads deep into the blossoms. This activity smears the upper part of their bodies with yellow pollen, giving them a temporary coloration never seen in bird books. When the fertilized

123

flowers of the saguaro turn into brilliant red fruits, the pollen-covered doves then become stained with crimson and at this season of the year even the nestlings show by their purplish-red color that saguaro fruits are their main food.

With surface water always a scarce commodity on the desert, any clue—even though faint—which points toward its location has value, not only to the early Indian residents but also to the prospectors, hunters, and outdoorsmen that roam the regions at the present time. Many animals are an aid in locating water. The following of a game trail which is joined by others, continuing in the same direction, has saved a number of human lives. Noticing an increase in the numbers of small birds in one special area can be used as a clue to the nearness of water. Even the pin-pointing of the flights of bees will serve as a lead. These, however, are all short-range clues, rarely usable unless the water is within a few miles of a thirsty traveler.

But the dove most adapted to desert living, the whitewing, has been known to lead men to water over a distance of twenty-five miles. If a knowledge of their habits and a timetable of their scheduled two trips a day for water had been known to some of the people lost on deserts, survival could have been prolonged until help arrived. The flights that these birds make for water occur at dawn and dusk and begin when four or five birds fly into the air at once. After circling for a moment while being constantly joined by others, they then set a direct course to some distant spot. A hurried trip to either side of their line of flight will show other flocks joining into the same formations and heading in the same general direction. If these two observations show courses almost parallel, then the water hole destination is many miles distant. But if the lines of flight converge rapidly, their spot of joining is the place where water should be found.

Chapter 9

Mammals of the Desert

We know of the mobility of birds, which makes possible their reaching water from almost any area in a matter of minutes, so we are not surprised when we encounter them miles from anywhere. But when mammals are observed in the same desolate regions, we begin to wonder. It is inconceivable that any creatures that depend on four legs could travel long distances through the desert, even if water in its free or surface form is available to sustain them. Some of the questions that baffled desert travelers early in the century were unanswerable until recently, when it was determined that water, as human beings use it, had only minor importance to most mammals that were adjusted to desert living.

To uncover one of these mysteries of waterless survival, some illuminating experiments were made on kangaroo rats—small desert animals that exist in the most arid regions. Some of their chosen homes are areas that receive rainfall only once in several years, where the humidity is so low that it supplies almost no dampness, and where fog is unknown. The sparse plants that are

125

found where the kangaroo rats live are annuals, growing, flowering, and dying only after the infrequent rains—so even a bit of shade is not available for the rodents. Yet the rats live and thrive, deliberately picking these spots in preference to others that seem to offer so much more.

The duplication of such an environment was not especially difficult for laboratory technicians. All they had to do was to eliminate moisture in any form, bring the heat up to about one hundred degrees in the daytime, cool it slightly at night, and feed the animals the dried twigs, seeds, and other bits of things that might be found in such a location. The rats were weight-checked when caught and then weighed at specified periods thereafter, on the theory that a loss of weight would mean a loss of body moisture—while a gain would signify the opposite.

In a general way those rodents kept in pens with a floor of deep sand maintained their weights, but those with shallow sand restricting the depths of their burrows had a tendency to lose weight. This suggested that food consumption was not the only factor in body moisture maintenance. When the deep burrows were examined it was found that the rats, on retiring, plugged the entrances. Thus what little moisture exuded from them

built up a humidity which tended to prevent more losses throughout the day.

Another experiment concerned their foods. Those on a diet of protein lost weight if they were not given water to drink, but those almost limited to carbohydrates for food maintained themselves in the same condition that they were when caught.

This was a partial proof of what scientists had suspected— that these animals are proficient in combining two gases, the hydrogen derived from carbohydrates and the oxygen taken from the air, in the right percentages to produce water. However, this internal laboratory making liquid cannot keep up with their bodies' needs unless other rigid conditions for strict water conservation are adhered to. The habit of closing the sleeping burrow, the trait of foraging only in the cool of the night, the ability to go into a lethargic sleep of estivation which slows down bodily functions—all are vitally important to make this unusual metabolism work. And, as an added safeguard to water conservation, their body wastes were extruded in an almost non-liquid form.

Many of the small animals that live on deserts are capable of manufacturing some metabolic water but most of them, unlike some kangaroo rats, will drink surface water when it is available. Other small rodents usually live where there is some plant growth, since desert plants generally store water. The pack rat trait of mixing green vegetation with dead organisms in the maintenance of their bulky houses is thought to create a humidity within which limits dehydration. And, as they often place their homes in exposed locations without the benefit of shade, the moisture evaporation from the greens probably has a cooling effect within.

If one of these mounds is carefully dissected, almost anything that can move under its own power or can be moved by the rat may be uncovered. The insects and arachnids that roam the deserts at night take daytime refuge in the mass of debris, and the lizards of the day shift seek these rodent homes as havens during the hours of darkness. In this twenty-four hour integrated occupancy, there are also larger reptiles. Nocturnal rattlesnakes are to be found in daylight, diurnal racers after dark. These last two animals find the nests protective comfort and a chance for a meal of pack rat.

As a source for inanimate objects, if they are near human habitation, the nests can be treasure-troves for the recovery of trinkets lost long ago. Pack, or trade, rats as their names imply, are continually moving objects from place to place. They rarely make a journey of more than a few feet without carrying something in their mouths. It might be a bit of cholla picked up as an addition to the mound. It might be a bone from a dead animal, or a feather molted by a passing bird. If, however, when so loaded they encounter something with more allure—they will drop the first choice and pick up that which they feel is better. Shiny objects are their favorites and, as a result, car keys, wrist watches, and coins have all found their way to their homes. If a complete list of these "finds" were ever to be compiled it would take a good-sized pawnshop window to display them.

In choice of habitats every species of desert rodent has its special requirements. The kangaroo rats will settle for a life on barren dunes. The versatile pack rat prefers areas with more plant growth, perhaps because there is more junk to pick up.

In between these two extremes of country there is a transitional zone, an area where sandy dust covers the ground but where growth is neither dense nor sparse.

Here the round-tailed ground squirrels make their homes and, almost like that group of plants roughly termed "evaders," survive the rigors of the desert by hibernating in the winter and estivating through the drier months of summer. Their combined daytime appearances probably occupy less than half the days in a year. When it is realized that about half of these active hours are broken by a nightly sleep, their time awake occupies a surprisingly low fraction of their total life.

During the rains and cold spells of winter which occur in the Tucson, Arizona, area—round tails are absent from the surface of the ground, remaining curled up in their burrows in hibernation. In this torpid state they are not only difficult to awaken but their heart and respiratory systems are so slowed down that they appear almost dead. Naturally, with bodily functions subdued, they use up less energy and can go for months without food.

With the warm days of spring they awaken, venture to the surface, and start scrounging food from the plants within a hundred-foot radius of their burrows. Their bodies, emaciated after their long fast, fill out rapidly, and when equipped with sufficient fatty tissue to support another sleep they even store some of the non-perishable food in their burrows. As temperatures rise their surface visits are shortened and shortly limiting these to a few minutes morning and evening, the creatures disappear underground once more. This stay, akin to hibernation which is caused by cold, is termed estivation—thought to be induced by the heat and the lack of humidity.

July brings the summer rains. When the humid air filters through the soil to the underground dens the rodents dig themselves out, sometimes followed by several young. They—like the bears—occasionally give birth to their young before coming to the surface. Again there is that hurried hunt for food, now much easier to find than in the spring, for the rains have

awakened dormant seeds and hastened them to growth. This abundance, uncommon through most of the year, builds more layers of fat on the skinny bodies, making these miniature prairie dogs—the round tails—ready for their next cyclic sleep.

There is another phase in their lives, their reproduction cycle. This is not only the key to the continued existence of the species but also to the lives of those predators which prey upon them. The average litter of all three of these rodents seems to be about four young at a time, and as pregnant female kangaroo rats have been found in ten of the twelve months of the year, there is a good possibility that they have from four to six broods each season. Baby pack rats usually appear in groups of three or four, and reasonable estimates place the number of litters per season at three. Round-tailed ground squirrels have about six young at a time and seem limited to one or possibly two broods per season. When all the time they spend sleeping is taken into consideration this small reproduction rate is reasonable, sufficient to maintain their population, which is subject to real danger only during their active hours.

If a pair of each of these rodents were to have a perfect survival of all young in a single year, there would be thirty or more kangaroo rats, nine or more pack rats, and eight or more round-tailed ground squirrels. If the original parents have a productive life of at least five years (they all live longer in captivity), the number of young produced should be multiplied by five. And, as most small rodents can produce young within a year, they would pair off and start their own overpopulation. In a very few years the world would be covered with them and thus become unlivable. That is why predatory animals are vitally important in the ecological balance of any region.

There are no predators that are strictly desert dwellers. Most of them, in order to earn their livelihood in the scheme of nature, must be nomadic—possessing the ability to move from place to place wherever food is above its normal abundance. And as soon as they have depleted the available food supply they move on, perhaps back to the areas recently vacated where their fast breeding prey has now increased beyond normal.

An example of such a predator is the coyote, a doglike creature who used to live almost exclusively on the deserts of the West. Now, however, they have moved into Alaska and parts of Canada, areas where they were formerly unknown. Their northward migration or expansion is a good example of why naturalists the world over abhor bounties on any living creature.

Early in the century the wolves of the Far North were thought to harm the other animals that man himself wished to kill. Bounties were inaugurated and the systematic slaughter of the giant dogs commenced. Guns, traps, and poison were all used in the campaign and within a score of years the wolves were practically exterminated. With them almost gone, the animals upon which they normally fed increased, a situation drawing predators from other regions, which in turn left a parallel vacuum in the areas they had vacated. So there was a chain reaction down the West Coast which resulted in a northward movement, and now the adaptable coyotes, animals of the deserts and plains, are filling the gap caused by man's interference.

There are many other examples of the inherent need for predators. One much closer to home concerns a group of ranchers in Colorado and their feud with the predatory animal control department of the United States Government. The argument concerns coyotes and jack rabbits. In years past the coyotes occasionally took young sheep or perhaps even weak or sickly calves. Whenever this occurred the control men moved in and with the wholesale use of poison and traps practically eliminated coyotes from the region. This saved some sheep and some calves but as a side effect it allowed rabbits to take over the range and destroy the valuable grasses. So it was a constant battle, with the scale of balance made to tilt stupidly one way and then the other. But in the past few years an order from all ranchers involved has banned killing coyotes and that section of the plains is now sensibly back to normal.

Another vital service performed by predatory animals is their taking of the weak or diseased. This not only eliminates an unwanted surplus that might start the spread of disease, but in leaving the alert and strong as breeders, the predators actually improve bloodlines of the species that are preyed upon. Before the days of telescopic sights and high-powered rifles, hunting probably performed a somewhat similar service, but now, with stalking at close range no longer necessary, most hunters pick the fittest and leave the others to propagate the race.

The taking of unfit deer was demonstrated by a pair of mountain lions in Tucson Mountain Park a few years ago, where the Desert Museum maintains a photographic blind at a water hole. Museum members often spend a night photographing deer, peccaries, or any other animals that come in to drink the water which is only ten feet from the observation windows. Until the pair of mountain lions moved in and made some kills (over a dozen actually counted), some of the water hole animal visitors were not healthy. In fact some were so thin due to old-age or ailments that photographers withheld recording them on film. After the lions had moved to other areas there was a noticeable reduction in the number of deer that visited the blind, but also notable was the absence of those formerly seen that had passed their prime.

The trait of the mountain lions which made them move on after they have caught the oldest or weakest of their prey seems common to most predators and particularly to badgers. When one or more badgers are in a neighborhood they make their presence known by attempting to dig out every rodent burrow they encounter. Some of these badger excavations leave piles of dirt a foot high and a yard wide, with a gaping hole downward that measures eight inches in diameter. When these are to be seen it usually signifies a successful mission by the badger and unsuccessful for the rodents pursued. Other excavations of burrows that were made by craftier or luckier rodents show a blockade made of a "Y" of roots, or a jumble of rocks, that effectively prevented the further entrance of the digging animal.

The seemingly tireless energy of badgers is unbelievable. Their necessary quota of food for a day probably consists of from four to six rodents of pack rat size. To obtain such a number they are usually forced to move almost a yard of dirt. They have a hard time getting prey, in spite of their sharing with pocket gophers the honor of being the most proficient diggers in the West. Their bodies, about three feet in length, are twice as wide as they are high. They are equipped with extremely muscular legs ending in two-inch-long claws, and are covered with a loose flexible hide. This extreme flexibility, in combination with one of the most muscular jaws in the animal world, makes them mean adversaries. Few dogs, even those trained for battle, ever win a badger-dog encounter.

Those that occasionally visit and drink at the wild life photographic blind stay in the area for about two weeks. In this space of time they will have tried every rodent burrow within a quarter-mile of the water hole and will have eaten a good percentage of the local rodent population. When their "pickings" become poor, however, they move on to other areas and there they start digging again. One individual visited the blind for short periods every two months, giving rise to the supposition that badgers may have four or five stopover places, probably set in a rough circle, which they use as a lifetime route.

Chain of command, a phrase so often heard in military jargon, also exists among the lower forms of animals. The mouse is afraid of the weasel, the weasel is afraid of the fox, the fox is afraid of the coyote—right on up the line. Generally speaking, power is a function of size, but there are a few interesting exceptions that exist in desert wild life. The underslung badger is one, the skunk another, while the forty-pound peccary or wild pig of the desert virtually rules them all. Simultaneous viewings of such diversified animals would be difficult in most areas but the shortage of water on deserts brings many non-compatible creatures momentarily together at the rare water holes. If human beings are watching, the caste systems of animals within a species, or of mixed species, may be observed.

Birds flock to the water hole during the daytime as well as

occasional cottontails, jack rabbits, and small ground squirrels. Competition is not a problem as most of the daytime visitors await their turn to drink. But as dusk approaches and the whitewings from distant valleys converge in increasing numbers, the rabbits move off and let the doves take over. These birds drink hurriedly, in a manner unlike most feathered creatures, for they insert the bill in the liquid and suck the water in as a continuous stream. The moment they have had enough, the doves take off and soon all are gone. Then from fifty feet away there comes the crunching sound of gravel made by sharp hooves on the well-worn trails—signals that deer are approaching, waiting only for darkness to get their first drink of the day.

These deer come in groups of four, six, or a dozen, milling about and often, like lines of people at a ticket window, pushing into the lead. Occasionally in this jostling for pole position, the one being nudged will break from the ranks. If his route takes him nearer the water, the group follows—if away from the water, his position is lost and he rejoins at the end of the line. Bucks, does, and fawns all appear at once during certain months of the year but throughout most seasons the bands are usually restricted to one sex or the other. Strangely in the mixed groups the bucks with antlers are the shy ones, and if there is a recognized leader it is an old doe or a female with young. After many false advances over the last fifty feet, drinking finally starts, usually initiated by an impatient fawn, followed immediately by all the others. When poolside space becomes crowded, fights for position commence, but in these inter-species squabbles the antlers of the buck are never used. Instead it is the slashing front feet of a deer standing on hind legs that drum on the back of another until it shifts its position to make room.

Sometimes when deer are drinking, a coyote, fox, or bobcat will come near, sit on haunches and await their departure. This bothers the does with small fawns. With ears down they will occasionally charge, rising to their hind legs when a few yards away. A buck disturbed by their presence, however, will advance with horns down—which is presumably the same pose used

136

when fighting another buck. Either type of attack seems to be more of a keep-your-distance warning than an actual desire for combat. Both are treated with disdain by the predators, who usually stand up, wander a few yards away, and sit down again. The approach of a skunk is a different matter. Skunks bluff their way forward with tail held high and front feet stamping. Occasionally a deer will try a bluff also, laying ears back and gingerly advancing. However, in every case witnessed, caution has overcome valor and the hoofed animal reluctantly retreats, while the skunk—small in size but equalized with a most potent weapon—takes his drink in peace.

Peccaries, the wild pigs of the desert, are its most arrogant inhabitants. They grunt, rattle stones, and occasionally even squeal when approaching the water holes. The furtiveness possessed by other animals seems to be entirely missing from their make-up. Perhaps one of the reasons for this is that their tooth and tusk equipment are murderous. The two lower tusks actually rub against others which point downward from the roof of the mouth, an action which sharpens all four to a razor-sharp edge. The mouth is capable of opening wide and the peccary method of fighting is to make upward slashes. Lassoed ones have been known to hamstring a horse before the lariat could be tightened to lift the pig off the ground. With such equipment peccaries can afford to be arrogant.

But most of the many publicized stories of their attacks on

human beings are highly exaggerated. There have been a few authentic cases of wounded or cornered pigs doing damage to human beings but in every case investigated the attacks were provoked. Even the start of the stories shows extreme exaggeration for they usually commence with a person being chased by a herd of pigs until he climbed up a tree. A knowledge of peccary country, as well as a memory of the extreme speed their short legs can generate, makes such an opening ridiculous. There is no man living that they can't outrun, and as for their habitat —it is jumbled rocks interspersed with thorny cacti. Trees of climbable size are many hundreds of feet apart and even these human havens have their trunks and branches covered with thorns.

Another contributing factor to the start of these tall tales might be due to the poor eyesight of the pigs and their habit of lying in any available shade during the extreme heat of a summer day. When bedded down, the coarse hair covering their bodies blends to the background, and as long as they remain motionless they are difficult to detect. At the slightest disturbance, however, they scatter like a covey of quail in every direction. Possibly only one of the entire sleeping group had detected the approach of a man, and all the rest—panicked by his single explosive grunt of danger—did not know where the danger was. Every escape path was used and perhaps one of the paths carried a pig or two within a few feet of a petrified person who supposed he was being attacked. And that is how the stories grew.

Chapter 10

The Balanced Community

By late June the desert is a parched land. The scarce water holes are reduced to dampness. The robust cacti, having used their stored water, show shriveled stems. The whitewing doves are flying longer distances to get their hurried drink. The drought-resistant trees have shed their leaves to retain what little moisture their trunks still have stored, and the temperatures soar to the point where a midday of less than one hundred degrees is considered cool. This heat, causing the drought, is about to break it, for the rising hot air—pushing ever upward—causes whatever moisture there is in the air to condense into clouds. They dissipate at night and reform the next day and after each twenty-four hour cycle the clouds are a little heavier than they were before.

Then comes the deluge, not widespread like the gentle winter rains, but spotty—wetting a square mile here and a square mile there. What is missing in coverage, however, is made up in volume, for these rains are cloudbursts—often limiting visibility to less than a hundred feet. Rivers that have been dry for months

become raging torrents, and flash floods, sweeping a six-foot wall of water over dips in the road, pick up luckless cars and can bury them in sand. Every depression becomes a pocket for water and in its slow seepage underground it not only softens the dirt but awakens a half-dozen species of amphibians to a short but active season. These animals are the most unusual of all desert residents.

An amphibian is a vertebrate that spends part of its life on land with lungs, but gets its start in life in water—breathing with gills. Salamanders, frogs, and toads fit into this narrow category. With but few exceptions, salamanders and frogs are confined to the permanently damp areas bordering rivers and lakes, or in forests where the humidity is high and there is perpetual dampness. Toads, too, inhabit such areas but ages ago some among them were pioneers that left their typical homes and learned to live in drier spots. This change of habitat necessitated drastic changes to permit survival. That they were eminently

successful is proven by the millions that appear on the surface of the desert on the night of the first summer rain.

After the violence of the day's storm hopping objects can be seen near rain pools. Some are only an inch in length, but others, olive-green in color, are as round and about the size of an indoor softball. All are heading downhill amid a din of hundreds of differently pitched voices. Some of the voices are high, almost painful to the human ear, while others are whistles, gasps, and grunts. Each different voice represents a different species. But the notes hold allurement for amphibians.

The shallows of the rain pool's shore lines are dotted with vocalizing creatures. A balloon-like membrane inflates under the chin and then suddenly collapses. Although that individual call is lost in the surrounding racket, it reaches the airways and is received by a female whose ears are attuned to the sound. With leisurely strokes of her slightly webbed hind feet, she swims toward the vocalist.

145

Pairings are occurring everywhere now. And as more toads —slow in digging their way to the surface of the ground— continue to arrive, romance is king for the next few days. Everything is hurried as well it might be—for haste in reproduction is the key to their ability to live on a desert.

By contrast, in a fresh-water swamp on the eastern seaboard, the jugerum calls of bullfrogs are heard on warm summer nights and somewhere in their homes of permanent water the tapioca-like eggs of this amphibian are slowly hatching. Weeks after being laid, tiny pollywogs emerge and their black bodies dot the shallow shore line. But their growth is slow, barely attaining half size when winter makes them lethargic. Spring finds them on the move once more. Their bodies widen, tails shorten, and hind legs break through the skin, but still there is no hurry to develop lungs in place of gills, for the water is always there. Finally, well into their second year, they transform into creatures that can hop on land.

But on the desert—the spadefoot toad, much smaller than its eastern cousin—speeds up the process. Although its production of offspring follows the same general pattern, its tempo is tuned for desert survival, and the rain pools in which these toads deposit their eggs have a habit of evaporating in a very few weeks. Wiggling black forms appear in the gelatinous mass of eggs the day after they are laid, and a few hours later the young emerge. Algae in the water supplies plentiful food, and within a week the hind legs push through the skin. In another week the young emerge as fully formed toads—for their first venture on land.

Fourteen days compared to fourteen months or more is an astounding variation for creatures that belong to the same family, but the lack of water can force some strange changes in the wild kingdom of the desert. Even after these baby toads have barely escaped the complete evaporation of the pool in which they were born, their lives are hurried. The same rain which made their parents dig their way to the surface, also stimulated the development of insects—so food was plentiful. But before much growth is attained the summer rains end and the dehydrating air starts drying the skins which must be kept moist. So the baby toads go underground. Some find ready-made holes under rocks, or use the deserted burrows of small rodents. Others, not so lucky, are forced to dig their own and the peculiar hind leg appendages—from which the name "spadefoot" is derived—are put to use as miniature shovels. For the next ten months their hurrying ceases as they sleep through part of the fall, all of winter and spring, and emerge again only when awakened by the torrential rainy season of the following summer.

The rest of the desert toads follow the same pattern in their yearly lives, but none is as highly developed for hasty breeding as the spadefoots. As though to compensate for a possible loss of offspring due to evaporation, the others usually seek larger and deeper pools, and one—the Colorado River toad—is partial to the permanent water of horse troughs or running streams when they are available.

Toads as a family are rarely preyed upon by other animals. This immunity to attack, not possessed by frogs, is due to glands situated just under the skin, making them distasteful to most predators. The Colorado River toad, largest member of the group native to the United States, has these glands developed to extremes, so much so that the main ones situated back of the head create rectangular bumps an inch in length and a quarter-inch high. These toads are more than just distasteful, for foolish puppies that have playfully attacked the giant amphibians have been known to die in less than an hour. Non-domesticated animals leave them strictly alone; whether instinctively or due to memory of a past indiscretion is not known.

Several centuries ago and throughout preceding ages, the summer rains had a more lasting and beneficial effect on the deserts than they do at present. During the 1700s when the San Xavier Mission was founded, many hillsides of the region had grass growing between the larger desert plants. Spots along the now-dry Santa Cruz River and its tributaries were marshes, having occasional pools which made possible the existence of

beaver, otter, ducks, and squawfish. The latter sometimes reached a length of fifty-two inches. In the driest of months in those bygone days, underground water was usually available just a mere ten feet from the surface. The grass on the hillsides, the lack of cattle trails, and many other factors prevented the occurrence of flash floods as we know them today. And, without the flash floods there were no deep erosion gullies except for those that formed the banks of legitimate rivers. The natural balance of the area, undisturbed either by man or his domesticated animals, kept the summer rain water from making its mad dash toward the sea. Instead it soaked into the ground, eventually reaching the underground water table that is now being drained at an alarming rate.

But by 1880 the desert started to show deterioration, enough to alarm the residents. Newspapers of the day mentioned the sudden formation of gullies, the lack of grass growth in certain valleys, and the spasmodic drying of some springs and wells which formerly had plenty of water. The clear stream of the Santa Cruz became muddy and the squawfish, food of the Papago Indians and mission personnel, became scarce—unable to live in the silt-laden waters which were carrying increasing amounts of topsoil with each flash flood. Woodcutters, most of whom lived along waterways, worked near home, and river trees were the first to go. Then beavers had no material to build dams. This eliminated the beavers, most important of all animals in the conservation of water through the dry season. When their dams disappeared, the otter, the ducks, and other water dependent creatures were forced to vacate.

Meanwhile the grassy valleys which had formerly been mowed for hay became the forced home for thousands of Mexican cattle (an estimated twelve million in a little over half a century). The first of these herds fed on the waving green blades, but each successive herd worked lower down on the grass and finally even the roots disappeared. With this change in habitat the Sonoran antelope, now listed as an endangered species, was forced out. With them went the masked bobwhite, a bird discovered in the

1880s and exterminated from the State of Arizona by 1912. This short period probably sets some sort of record of annihilation but not one that human beings should be proud of.

This paints a dismal picture, a picture of a once balanced biotic community that has changed considerably. But generally speaking, where one animal has been forced out, the vacuum caused by his departure has been filled by another. So an ecology has been maintained, not necessarily the one that took ages to form by nature's pattern—but workable nevertheless. And even when our overpopulation forces additional changes, there are always the National Parks and Monuments maintained "in unimpaired form" and for the "benefit of future generations." These sanctuaries can bring us back to the desert, that strange weather-created area that is an interesting, necessary, and integral part of the wild kingdom.

Index

R. MARLIN PERKINS, the commentator and star of the weekly television program *Wild Kingdom*, is the Director of the world-famous St. Louis Zoological Gardens. His career began at this same St. Louis Zoo, where his first job was as a laborer—sweeping sidewalks and trimming hedges. He rose rapidly to become Curator of Reptiles, and was then offered the position as Curator of the zoo in Buffalo, New York. From Buffalo, he moved to Chicago, where he was the Director of the Lincoln Park Zoo.

His television career started in Chicago, where he was the star of the program *Zoo Parade*. After his return to St. Louis in 1962, Mr. Perkins started *Wild Kingdom*, a program that has won countless awards, including the coveted Emmy.

LEWIS WAYNE WALKER, the author of *Survival Under the Sun*, is presently the Associate Director of the Arizona-Sonora Desert Museum at Tucson, Arizona. Previously he was with The American Museum of Natural History in New York City and for a while he was Curator of Exhibits at the San Diego, California, Zoo.

He has written over two thousand articles which have appeared in almost all the natural history and nature magazines of this country. To supplement his writings, and as his hobby, Mr. Walker is an avid photographer. He is married and lives in Tucson, Arizona.